D1384033

WITHDRAWN

A Defence of
History and Class Consciousness

A Defence of
History and Class Consciousness

Tailism and the Dialectic

GEORG LUKÁCS

Translated by Esther Leslie

With an introduction by John Rees
and a postface by Slavoj Žižek

CALVIN T. RYAN LIBRARY
U. OF NEBRASKA AT KEARNEY

VERSO

London • New York

This edition first published by Verso 2000
© Verso 2000
Translation © Esther Leslie 2000
Introduction © John Rees 2000
Postface © Slavoj Žižek 2000
First published as *Chvostismus und Dialektik*, by Áron Verlag, Budapest, 1996
© Erben von Georg Lukács 1996

All rights reserved

The moral rights of the authors and translator have been asserted

Verso
UK: 6 Meard Street, London W1V 3HR
USA: 180 Varick Street, New York, NY 10014–4606

Verso is the imprint of New Left Books

ISBN 1–85984–747–1

British Library Cataloguing in Publication Data
A catalogue record for this book is available from the British Library

Library of Congress Cataloging-in-Publication Data
Lukács, György 1885–1971.
 [Chvostismus und Dialektik. English]
 A defence of history and class consciousness: tailism and the
 dialectic/Georg Lukács; translated by Esther Leslie; with an
 introduction by John Rees and a postface by Slavoj Zizek.
  p. cm.
 ISBN 1–85984–747–1 (cloth)
 1. Socialism. 2. Proletariat. 3. Capitalism. 4. Communism.
 5. Class consciousness. 6. Dialectical materialism. 1. Title.

HX260.5.A6L78313 2000
335.4'112—dc21

00–028980

Typeset by M Rules
Printed by Biddles Ltd, Guildford and King's Lynn

Contents

Editorial note

Throughout the text, references to *History and Class Consciousness* (abbreviated as HCC) give page numbers for the 1971 edition translated by Rodney Livingstone.

Elsewhere, where possible, references to works of Lenin and Marx and Engels refer to the English-language editions of their *Collected Works* (abbreviated respectively as CW and MECW and followed by the volume and page numbers).

Introduction

John Rees

The document contained in this book has been a secret for more than seventy years. Written in 1925 or 1926, it appears here in English for the first time.[1] Its existence was unknown, never referred to by Georg Lukács in any of the numerous accounts and interviews that he gave about his life. But if the very existence of this book is surprising, its contents are even more so. Here Georg Lukács defends his masterpiece, *History and Class Consciousness*, from the attacks made on it after its publication in 1923. That an author should defend his work is not very unusual. But Lukács was not engaged in a commonplace literary debate. In the Communist movement of the mid-1920s the forces of Stalinism were growing more powerful. To confront them might mean losing a great deal more than one's reputation. Lukács is always supposed not to have done so. Much of the great critical industry that has subsequently grown around Lukács's work has assumed that the perspective of *History and Class Consciousness* lasted no longer than the following year, 1924, and the publication of Lukács's *Lenin: A Study in the Unity of his Thought*. But here we have the proof that Lukács continued to defend *History and Class Consciousness* into the mid-1920s.

The defence that Lukács mounts here will also overturn some received opinion about the meaning of *History and Class Consciousness*. It has frequently been assumed that Lukács's critics were right when they accused *History and Class Consciousness* of being hostile to the idea that Marx's method could be extended to account for developments in the natural world. That myth is laid to rest in the passages that follow. It has also often been assumed that the issue of revolutionary organisation was not an integral part of Lukács's recovery of Marx's theory of alienation. That too is a view that will now have to be abandoned. But before we look more closely at the theoretical issues raised by his work, we need to look at Georg Lukács and the path he travelled to revolutionary socialism.

Georg Lukács's path to Marxism

To have met Georg Lukács in the mid-1920s when he wrote his defence of *History and Class Consciousness* would have been to meet a revolutionary exile. Lukács had fled to Vienna from his native Hungary after the fall of the Workers' Republic that lasted from March until August 1919. He had been a political commissar in the republic, at first for education and then also with the Fifth Division of the Red Army. After the counter-revolution he remained in Hungary to reorganise the Communist Party. Had the military regime of Admiral Horthy, which had taken power with the help of France, Britain and other Western powers, caught him, he would have been executed, as was his co-worker Otto Korvin. What made the son of one of Budapest's wealthiest bankers become a revolutionary willing to face exile and risk death?

From his early teenage years Lukács found himself driven between two ideological poles. On the one hand he reacted against the semi-feudal aristocratic environment of the Austro-Hungarian Empire. He admired modern drama, Ibsen in particular. 'By the age of fifteen,' Lukács recalled, 'I had arrived at what was for the time an extremely avant garde Western position.' He was influenced by sociological and cultural theories in Germany, where he studied later in the pre-war decade. Of his political aspirations at this time Lukács says, 'I wanted to change things . . . my ambition was to bring about changes in the old Hungarian feudal system. But there was no question of turning these wishes into political activity because there was no movement along those lines in Budapest at the time.'[2]

On the other hand, Lukács's hostility to the old order in Hungary did not transform him, as it did many other radicals and liberals from his background, into an uncritical supporter of Germany or the Western democracies. Despite the fact that he mostly lived in Heidelberg from 1912 until the end of the war, and that he originally went to Germany with the intention of becoming a 'German literary historian', Lukács soon came to 'the realisation that the history of German thought contained a fair measure of conservatism'.[3] In short, Lukács says, 'For all my condemnation of conditions in Hungary, this did not mean that I was prepared to accept English Parliamentarianism as an alternative ideal.'[4]

This double rejection of the political alternatives offered by contemporary society was matched by a rejection of the intellectual alternatives available in pre-war Germany. The empirical sciences and positivist philosophy were one, dominant, trend in Germany as the fruits of industrialisation and imperial conquest shaped ideology. But these trends collided with an older romantic and idealist consciousness that, while not progressive in all its forms, was sceptical of the new utilitarian, scientistic attitudes. Lukács came into contact with some of the foremost representatives of this ideological resistance to the dehumanising, materialistic drive of commodity capitalism, such as the neo-Kantian Heidelberg philosophers Rickert and Windelband. What drew Lukács to these thinkers was their attempt to rescue some role for consciousness and human action from under the wheels of the deterministic juggernaut of positivist science. As Rodney Livingstone has noted: 'It should be noted that these neo-Kantian and parallel attempts to defend the autonomy of spirit avoided having recourse to explicitly metaphysical or religious positions. Inevitably, therefore, the place of religion was often taken by art. Lukács shared in this fashionable aestheticism for a time . . . it involved him in a search for authenticity amidst the sterility of modern life.'[5]

One possible source of a solution to the social and intellectual contradictions of modern life, the workers' movement, seemed no solution at all to Lukács at this time. The German Social Democratic Party (SDP), the most powerful of the labour parties gathered in the Second International, was a vast bureaucracy, a 'state within a state' which seemed to reproduce exactly those elements of modern society that

Lukács opposed. In Karl Kautsky, the leading theoretician of the Second International, Lukács simply saw another expression of the positivistic determinism that he rejected.

But this rejection of the materialistic culture of modern life left Lukács caught in a paradox. In a world characterised as a realm of 'absolute sinfulness', from where could progress come? From what point on the social horizon could there originate a force capable of leading beyond these two inadequate alternatives? Lukács had no answer to these questions. And, finding no social force or political strategy equal to the task, his mind turned to artistic and ethical responses. Perhaps brief moments of artistic experience might overcome the alienation from modern political forms. Perhaps there might be an ethical stance that would allow one to withstand the degrading experience of living in a society where corruption was not simply excess but a fundamental principle of life. Lukács himself described this attitude as 'romantic anti-capitalism'. It is from this pre-war period that two works of cultural criticism date, *The Soul and its Forms* (1911) and *The Theory of the Novel* (1916).

The outbreak of the First World War only deepened this paradox. 'The cultural elite into which he had assimilated showed that its contempt for contemporary German life was perfectly compatible with a chauvinistic posture,' notes Rodney Livingstone; 'The ideology of "non-political" thinkers and poets turned out to be conservative and nationalist in practice.'[6] Lukács's anti-capitalism inoculated him from this pro-war mood. But there was still no obvious home for him in the socialist movement since the support that the SDP gave to the war was a prime cause of despair. This is why the major socialist influences on Lukács up to this point were syndicalists such as Ervin Szabo who were beyond the pale of Second International Marxism.

Lukács explains how his views evolved during the war:

> The German and Austrian armies may well defeat the Russians and this will mean the overthrow of the Romanovs. That is perfectly in order. It is also possible that the German and Austrian forces will be defeated by the British and the French and that will spell the downfall of the Hapsburgs and the Hohenzollerns. That too is quite in order. But who will defend us against the western democracies?[7]

Thus the old dilemma was revisited, but with a new intensity. It was only resolved with the coming of the Russian Revolution. 'Only the Russian Revolution opened a window to the future; the fall of Czarism brought a glimpse of it, and with the collapse of capitalism it appeared in full view . . . we saw – at last! at last! – a way for mankind to escape war and capitalism.'[8]

Returning to Hungary in 1918, Lukács was one of the first to join the newly formed Communist Party. 'As far as Lukács was concerned the choice was made irrevocable towards the end of 1917,' writes István Mészáros; 'In the turmoil of the unfolding revolutions he committed himself for life not only to the Marxist perspective, but simultaneously also to what he considered to be its only feasible vehicle of realisation, the vanguard party.'[9] Lukács was by no means fully aware of the implications of Marx's theory, despite his early reading of *Capital*, Hegel and, during the war, Rosa Luxemburg's writings. But in this he was by no means alone among the leaders of the new party. Very little was known of Lenin's writings even among those, such as party leader Bela Kun, who returned from Russian prisoner-of-war camps. Yet, within a matter of months, the new party and its inexperienced leaders found themselves at the head of a workers' movement which took state power. In contrast, when the Bolsheviks led the Russian Revolution, they were veterans who had been constructing a revolutionary organisation since at least 1903. They had been shaped by the revolution of 1905, by the long years of recovery that followed the defeat of that revolution, by the struggle against the war. The Hungarian Communist Party had no such past to steel it, and this proved a decisive weakness in the dramatic course of the revolution.

The Hungarian Revolution

The year of the Hungarian Revolution, 1919, was the high point of the post-war revolutionary wave that swept through Europe. Hungary's Austrian neighbour was swept by revolutionary agitation and the short-lived Bavarian Soviet republic arose in Germany during the lifetime of the Hungarian Revolution. At the same time, the French Black Sea fleet mutinied. The Hungarian Revolution itself opened with a strike wave in January 1918. The wartime coalition government could not contain the unrest, despite the participation of the Hungarian SDP. A rail workers' general strike saw 150,000 on the streets of Budapest chanting 'Long live the workers' councils!' and 'Greetings to Soviet Russia!'. Only the resignation of the SDP executive got the strikers back to work. But strikers were soon back on the streets again. This phase of the movement culminated in a general strike that lasted from 22 June to 27 June when it was called off by the SDP. Nevertheless, the government buckled under this pressure and, in October 1918, the war cabinet collapsed and was replaced by an administration headed by the liberal Count Karolyi but which included SDP ministers.

This Autumn Rose Revolution, as it became known, produced a highly unstable situation. The Western victors of the First World War forced Karolyi to cede half of Hungarian territory, intensifying widespread shortages. In response, peasant uprisings and urban riots fused with industrial action. Workers' and soldiers' councils were formed and real power increasingly rested in their hands, not those of the government. 'The government,' records one historian, 'could not implement a single major decision . . . without the tacit or expressed consent of the socialists.'[10]

Yet these workers' councils were dominated by the SDP. Even in November 1918, the revolutionary left was still only a political club inside the SDP. The Hungarian Communist Party (HCP) was not formed until the following month. Lukács was an early member. The HCP grew rapidly in early 1919, but its inexperience showed itself almost immediately. An attempted insurrection in February 1919 led to repression, the closure of the HCP headquarters and the arrest of Bela Kun and many of its other leaders. Lukács, as a member of the 'replacement' leadership, became the effective editor of the party paper.

On 18 March several thousand steel workers voted to fight to free the HCP prisoners and the printers' union voted for a two-day strike against the government. The soldiers' council and the Budapest militia came under HCP control. But the decisive blow was struck by the Western powers. Their representative in Budapest, Colonel Vyx, handed the government a note on 19 March which demanded that the whole country, bar a 20-mile area around the capital, be put under military occupation. The government fell and handed power to an SDP administration. Hungary was once again at war, threatened by Romanian, Czech and French troops.

The new SDP government could be effective only if it could master working-class insurgency – and this was possible only if the SDP could master the HCP. On 21 March SDP leaders visited Bela Kun in jail and proposed a merger between their own party and the HCP. This was an entirely cynical manoeuvre on the part of the SDP who hoped that merging with the HCP would, in addition to taming the working class, bring Russian military assistance against the threat of Western occupation. As one SDP leader told the workers' council:

> We must take a new direction to obtain from the East what has been denied to us by the West . . . we shall announce to the whole world that the proletariat of this country has taken guidance of Hungary and at the same time offered its fraternal alliance to the Soviet Russian government.[11]

Nevertheless, Kun agreed to join this 'revolutionary government' and talked down opposition inside the HCP in a series of face-to-face meetings. The HCP was very much the junior partner in the government, controlling only a minority of the government offices. Even their own party apparatus was swallowed up by the SDP. Lukács fully supported this strategy.

The new government, relying on a massive mobilisation by workers' organisations, was successful in its initial campaign to defeat the Western armies sent against it. But its policy was wildly ultra-left in all essential matters. The Hungarian CP committed a series of errors that were the almost polar opposites of the choices made by the Bolsheviks in similar circumstances. Where the Bolsheviks gave the land to the peasants, the HCP nationalised it. 'In practice the new managers were often the former owners and little changed for the peasants and labourers who worked on the estates.' Understandably, as even official reports admitted, 'many villages have revolted' and 'where they are unable to rise openly the peasantry suffers our rule with grim fury'.[12] The Bolsheviks were cautious in their policy of nationalisation, until the onset of civil war forced their hand; the HCP tried to nationalise everything, down to the level of small shops, personal savings and even jewellery.[13]

Even this catalogue of errors might not have been fatal had the insurrectionary mood in neighbouring Austria resulted in revolution or had the Red Army operations in the Ukraine sustained themselves for long enough to threaten Romania from the east. But the Communist leadership in Vienna was every bit as inept as that in Budapest and the moment for an Austrian revolution passed away in what the British Foreign Office rightly described as 'opera bouffe'.[14] As the military situation turned in favour of the White armies in the Ukraine, the hope of military aid from Russia dwindled.

Bela Kun, however, still had one final error to contribute to the failure of the revolution. Where the Bolsheviks maintained an absolute distrust of the imperial powers, Bela Kun trusted the French president's assurances that troops could be simultaneously withdrawn by both sides. This final misjudgement, and the ensuing second advance by pro-Western troops, brought the fall of the workers' government and opened the door to Admiral Horthy's counter-revolution. Kun knew exactly who was to blame. In his final speech he said: 'No one will succeed in governing this country. The proletariat, which was discontented with our rule . . . was shouting in the factories loudly and in spite of all propaganda: "Down with the Dictatorship!".'[15] Kun fled immediately to Vienna while Lukács remained in Hungary to try to reform the shattered HCP underground. After two months in hiding, he too left for Vienna.

A Leninist in exile

It was only when Lukács arrived in his Vienna exile that he had his first real chance to study Lenin's writings. He was reading them not only against the background of the still unfolding Russian Revolution but also against his own experience in the defeated Hungarian Workers' Republic. It was under the impact of these combined experiences that Lukács finally settled accounts with his previous philosophical approach and completed his journey to revolutionary Marxism. But although Lukács's decision to join the HCP had been so sudden that he took many of his friends by surprise, his possession of a full understanding of Marxism was necessarily a slower and more uneven process.

Lukács brought many intellectual ghosts from his past with him as he became a Marxist. In 'Bolshevism as a Moral Problem', written in the same month that Lukács joined the HCP, he sought to analyse Bolshevism as if he were still answering the old problem of how a person can behave ethically in a totally sinful world. Lukács was responding to social-democratic accusations that the Bolshevik regime in Russia had not abolished class rule but merely replaced the dictatorship of the oppressors with that of the oppressed. Lukács does not respond with a concrete account of the difference between workers' democracy and bourgeois democracy. He does not even make the obvious point that the dictatorship of the majority over the minority is not, morally or in any other sense, the same as a dictatorship of a minority over the majority. Instead, he accepts the terms of the debate created by his opponents, asking whether good (a classless society) can be reached by bad means (dictatorship). 'Bolshevism rests on the metaphysical assumption that good can issue from evil, that it is possible . . . to lie our way to the truth. The present writer is not able to share this faith and therefore sees at the root of the bolshevik position an irresolvable moral dilemma.'[16]

All this is a universe away from Trotsky's later approach to the problem in *Their Morals and Ours*. The methodological crux of this difference is that Trotsky does not conceive the world as an absolutely corrupted environment in which any action has to reckon with contamination from its surroundings. Instead, he sees society as a contradictory reality in which the practical actions of different classes, sections of classes and their political representatives can be judged on the basis of their contribution towards ending exploitation and oppression. The difference in Lukács's and Trotsky's conclusions is striking. Lukács's conclusion leads to paralysis; Trotsky's to the idea that the means must be appropriate to ends, that lying and deception are not acceptable means of furthering the interests of a struggle that ultimately depends on the clarity of class consciousness among workers. Trotsky understands how the contradictions of capitalism can be exploited to advance the consciousness of workers. Lukács only sees the bald opposition of the already converted to the mass still caught in the coils of capitalist sinfulness.

Lukács's previous absolute hostility to capitalist society was initially transferred to the political stand that he took when he joined the HCP. This total rejection went far beyond the opposition, entirely justified in principle, to capitalist society shared by all revolutionaries and penetrated down to every strategic and tactical decision faced by the workers' movement. Participation in parliamentary institutions was rejected on grounds of principle and we have already seen that Lukács supported the ultra-left agrarian policy of the Hungarian CP. The international revolutionary wave that began in Russia, the revulsion of many working-class militants at the policies of the existing reformist parties, the rapid creation of mass communist parties headed by inexperienced leaders, meant that ultra-leftism was 'in the air'. Many others in the newly formed Communist International also held such views: Amadeo Bordiga in Italy, Sylvia Pankhurst in England and the Dutch 'council communists' Anton Pannekoek and Henriette Roland-Holst. It was against this trend that Lenin aimed his *Left-Wing Communism: An Infantile Disorder*. Lukács was initially distinguished from others in this current only by the rigour of his thought, by his insistence on resting his strategic conclusions on a line of reasoning running right back to the philosophical foundations of Marxism.[17]

In his essays of this time the old ethical framework competes with a newly acquired Marxist framework. In 'The Question of Parliamentarianism', for instance, Lukács adopts the standard ultra-left rejection of 'compromise' with the institutions of the capitalist state.[18] It was this article that Lenin specifically criticised in *Left-Wing Communism*. Lukács gradually relinquished these ultra-left attitudes as he studied Lenin and participated in the debates of the Third International, although even this was an uneven process. Lukács had already accepted Lenin's position on participation in parliamentary elections when *Left-Wing Communism* appeared. He first changed his attitude towards the domestic problems of the Hungarian revolution and only later fully abandoned his ultra-left attitudes towards the international problems of the Communist movement. The last vestiges are to be found in his qualified support for the German Communist Party's March Action in 1921. But, by the time he came to write *History and Class Consciousness* in 1922, he had left this transitional phase behind – and with it the unstable intellectual amalgam of Marxism and romantic anti-capitalism.

Some of the essays in *History and Class Consciousness* first appeared during Lukács's ultra-left period. But even these essays were significantly re-written for inclusion in *History and Class Consciousness*. The revisions, as Michael Löwy has shown, were designed to strip these essays of any remnants of ultra-leftism.[19] For instance, the most heavily revised piece, 'What is Orthodox Marxism?', although it is still dated 1919, has been re-written to include passages that read as a direct critique of Lukács's own position in the 1919 essay 'Bolshevism as a Moral Problem': 'Every attempt to rescue the "ultimate goal" or the "essence" of the proletariat from every impure contact with – capitalist – existence leads ultimately to the same remoteness from reality, from "practical, critical activity", and to the same relapse into the utopian dualism of subject and object, of theory and practice to which Revisionism has succumbed.'[20] Moreover, the most important essays in the book were new – 'Reification and the Consciousness of the Proletariat' and 'Towards a Methodology of the Problem of Organisation'. And it is in these essays, above all, that Lukács develops the most sustained account of alienation since Marx himself and then goes on to demonstrate how the nature of working-class consciousness so conceived provides the philosophical and sociological ground for the Leninist theory of the revolutionary party.

The meaning of *History and Class Consciousness*

The towering achievement of *History and Class Consciousness* is to have recovered the greater part of Marx's theory of alienation from the oblivion to which the theoreticians of the Second International had consigned it. Lukács rejected the view that class consciousness could simply be read off from economic circumstances. Instead, he argued that the combined effects of class location, the commodity structure of modern capitalism and the class struggle shaped class consciousness.

Lukács understood that the different positions occupied by the working class and the capitalist class in the production process shaped their differing attitudes towards exploitation and oppression. In this he did not depart from the Marxist orthodoxy as taught by the Second International. And, in so far as the consciousness of the capitalist class was concerned, there were fewer problems with this approach since their consciousness did seem to reflect their class position in a relatively straightforward way. But there are greater difficulties when we consider the consciousness of the working class. Workers frequently hold ideas that are supportive of, or at least compatible with, the capitalist system. It cannot therefore be said that their class position and their class interests are immediately reflected in their class consciousness. How were Marxists to explain this divergence between class position and class consciousness?

The orthodox Marxist reply had been to point to the role of the state, the press, the Church, the education system and other institutions in capitalist society as responsible for misleading workers as to their real interests. The solution was for the SDP to provide more socialist education, more electoral success and so on in order to act as a counter-weight. In so far as it went, this reply contained a good deal of truth. The institutions of capitalism certainly do try to influence workers' ideas in such a way that they become supporters of capitalism. And, certainly, socialist propaganda is one important counter-weight. Nevertheless, this reply alone will not do. After all, if such pro-capitalist arguments do not correspond at all to the class position of workers, why do they not simply reject them out of hand? And why do socialist ideas, since they correspond to the class position of workers, not simply spread like wildfire, no sooner heard than accepted?

Lukács looked more closely at the experience of workers under capitalism in order to find an answer. His essential point was that the transformation of labour power into a commodity, the very foundation of capitalist production, atomises workers and works to prevent them from grasping the nature of the system that exploits them. The capitalist system treats wage labour as something to be bought and sold on the market like any other commodity. This induces the sensation in workers that they are simply individual atoms whose fate is dependent on a force – the market – over which they have no control. And this is actually true in so far as workers remain isolated individuals attempting to get a job, maintain a decent wage and so on from the employing class. Indeed, this feeling of powerlessness in the face of the market is also an accurate reflection of reality in the additional sense that even the individual capitalist confronts a market over which he or she has very limited control. Thus capitalists are not wholly disingenuous when they say that they are only making job cuts or wage reductions as a result of the 'impersonal dictates of the market'. They simply forget to add that they are the beneficiaries of this mechanism.

In short, Lukács rediscovered the idea that a social construct, the market, appears to the actors trapped within it as a natural necessity which imposes a pattern on their lives in a manner that they are powerless to resist. In *History and Class Consciousness* Lukács calls this process 'reification', the freezing of an institution or ideology created by human beings into a force that controls human beings. This is precisely the idea of Marx's writings on alienation and commodity fetishism. From such feelings of powerlessness grow the deference to hierarchy, the acceptance of bureaucracy, the illusions of religion to which the orthodox accounts of workers' consciousness all pointed. But, in Lukács's hands, they are given a real grounding in the daily experience of workers under capitalism.

But if capitalist and worker alike suffer from the effects of alienation and commodity fetishism, does this not mean that any hope of resistance on the part of the working class is as unfounded as expecting capitalists to oppose their own system? Lukács thinks not, and his further investigations of what it means to reduce labour power to the status of a commodity shows why he still sees the possibility of working-class resistance. In any commodity transaction the buyer and the seller have equal rights. Sellers have the right to charge the price they think fit for their commodity and the buyers have the right to offer a price that they think fit. If they agree on a price, a commodity changes hands; if they do not, they walk away and that is the end of the matter. But labour power is a commodity of a different type. The sellers, the workers, can never be separated from their commodity, their labour power, no matter how much the buyers, the capitalists, might wish it. Consequently, the conflict over the price of labour, the duration and intensity of its use is never completed. And, if this conflict is simply viewed through the normal lens of capitalist ideology, then both the buyer and the seller have an equal right to conduct this struggle. Since this conflict cannot be resolved within the bounds of capitalist ideology, it resolves itself by means of class struggle. Such resistance on the part of the workers must also mark the beginning of an alternative conception of the world, a breach in the wall of alienation, the root of workers overcoming their sense of powerlessness. As Lukács writes:

> The instant this consciousness arises and goes beyond what is immediately given we find in a concentrated form the basic issue of the class struggle: the problem of force. For this is the point where the 'eternal laws' of capitalist economics fail and become dialectical and are thus compelled to yield up decisions regarding the fate of history to the conscious actions of men.[21]

This understanding of class consciousness has two important immediate consequences. First, it forces us to pay attention to the class struggle as a decisive element in the transformation of class consciousness rather than an exclusive emphasis on propaganda, which is one conclusion of the old social-democratic account of how class consciousness is formed. If bourgeois ideology begins to break down at the point where the relations of exploitation and oppression are challenged, then agitation and the practical leadership of the class struggle assume a renewed importance for socialists. Second, Lukács's approach does not commit the opposite error to the social-democratic theory by underestimating the importance of social institutions, political parties and ideologies in shaping class consciousness. For Lukács, workers' consciousness is shaped by two contradictory material experiences. On the one hand, he sees atomisation and alienation consequent on being treated as a commodity. On the other hand, there is the impulse to resistance imparted by the rightful exercise by the sellers of control over the conditions under which they will part with labour power. In these circumstances, the different institutional and ideological structures of society can help to resolve this contradiction by supporting either the progressive or the regressive pole. Unions and workers' parties may aid resistance and solidarity. The media, the education system and the institutions of the capitalist state may work to advance the feelings of powerlessness and atomisation that workers already suffer in the economic realm.

The second great achievement of *History and Class Consciousness* was to deduce the role that could be played by a revolutionary party in these circumstances. Since the whole commodity structure of capitalism creates a contradictory consciousness among workers, and since the battles that result from the fundamental economic conflict over the disposal of labour power are always uneven, it follows that some sections of workers become class conscious before others. The key to the role of the revolutionary organisation is that as many of these workers as possible should band together in a party in order to hasten the process by which their fellow workers also become class conscious. As Lukács puts it, 'the prevailing disunity, the differing degrees of clarity and depth to be found in the consciousness of the different individuals, groups and strata of the proletariat make the organisational separation of the party from the class inevitable'.[22]

The political impulse for this strategy was a reaction against the social-democratic model of the party that was, ideally, co-extensive with the class. It thus reproduced within the party all the compromises with the capitalist system that are an unavoidable part of working-class consciousness while it remained caught in the cage of alienated existence. But, in rejecting this approach, the opposite danger was posed – that the party would cut itself off in sectarian isolation from the class. Lukács was aware of this problem:

> Organisational independence is senseless and leads straight back to sectarianism if at the same time it does not constantly pay heed *tactically* to the level of consciousness of the largest and most retrograde sections of the masses . . . the ability to act, of self-criticism, of self-correction and of theoretical development all co-exist in a constant state of interaction. The Communist Party does not function as a stand-in for the proletariat even in theory.[23]

This combination of insights into the way in which class consciousness is formed and into the nature of the revolutionary party was unique. Lenin had arrived at the notion of a vanguard party under the practical pressures of Russian conditions and in opposition to the Mensheviks after the 1903 split in the Russian Social Democratic and Labour Party. But he had not thought these lessons of general significance until the bankruptcy of the social-democratic parties was exposed by their support for their own ruling classes in the First World War. Even then, this connection between the general nature of class consciousness and the role of the revolutionary party was not established with any great precision. Marx's theory of alienation was not deployed for these purposes and the continued existence of reformist consciousness of workers was ascribed to the malevolence of reformist leaders and the role of the 'aristocracy of labour', a grouping not clearly distinguished from the trade union bureaucracy. Much of Lenin's analysis was perfectly correct – with the exception of the role attributed to the 'aristocracy of labour' – but it did not explain why some workers followed bad leaders and how others, who did not, could act.

Lukács broke this theoretical log-jam. In so doing, he connected Lenin's theory of the party to the deepest roots of Marx's analysis of capitalism. And he did so in a way that revived Marx's dialectical method and counter-posed it to the determinism that provided the theoretical framework for pre-war social democracy. This was always likely to be a controversial project. Its sheer sweep was still highly unusual. Even those who had come down on the revolutionary side of the divide in the socialist movement in 1914 still owed much of their understanding of Marxism to the training that they had received from Karl Kautsky, Georgi Plekhanov and the other theoreticians of the Second International. Few had, like Lenin at the outset of the war, completely reappraised their understanding of the dialectic and the Hegelian heritage of Marxism. Consequently, Lukács's account of Marxism would have seemed unorthodox whenever it had appeared. It appeared all the more so in the climate that was then forming in the Communist International.

The attack on *History and Class Consciousness*

The environment in which *History and Class Consciousness* was launched in 1923 was not conducive to serious theoretical discussion. The debate began shortly after its publication and ran through the Fifth Congress of the Communist International in mid-1924. This was a decisive moment for the communist movement, coming after the defeat of the 'German October' and marking the further degeneration of the Russian Revolution. The year of *History and Class Consciousness*'s publication was the year when Lenin's illness excluded him from all political activity. It was the year of the first great assault by Stalin and Zinoviev on Trotsky's Left Opposition. The inner party crisis of this year was the first where *Pravda* became the mouthpiece of the party leadership and acted as a censor of opposing views within the party. The Bolshevik Party's January 1924 Thirteenth Conference and the May 1924 Congress, where international delegates were present, marked the first great defeats of the Left Opposition. In the wake of the Fifth Congress of the Communist International in June and July 1924, Trotsky launched his magnificent attack on Stalinism, *Lessons of October*. By the end of that year Stalin was, for the first time, propagating the theory of 'socialism in one country'.

But, if the international situation was unpropitious, so was the situation in Lukács's own Hungarian party. The weak and inexperienced leadership of the Hungarian Communist Party was in exile, and divided over their assessment of what had gone wrong with their revolution. Bela Kun's ultra-leftism remained unchecked even by his interview with Lenin on arrival in Russia – an encounter that resulted in Kun collapsing in the road outside the building where the interview took place. Victor Serge, the great independent-minded chronicler of the international revolution, knew the Hungarian émigrés. He held Lukács in 'greatest esteem' for his 'first class brain which could have endowed Communism with a true intellectual greatness' if Lukács had not ultimately come to terms with Stalinism. But, in Kun, Serge saw 'the incarnation of intellectual inadequacy, uncertainty of will, and authoritarian corruption'.[24]

Kun remained a firm favourite of Zinoviev, the president of the

Communist International. Zinoviev himself, while a long-time collaborator of Lenin during the period between the 1905 revolution and 1917, had opposed the October revolution. Victor Serge remembers Zinoviev at this time as 'simply a demagogue, a popularizer of ideas worked out by Lenin'. But Serge also saw that Zinoviev 'was obsessed by the error of judgement which had led him to oppose the incipient Bolshevik revolution; in consequence he had now swung into an authoritarian and exaggerated revolutionary optimism. "Zinoviev", we used to say, "is Lenin's biggest mistake".'[25] Lukács found himself in opposition to both these figures. In the Hungarian CP he joined the opposition led by Jeno Landler, a former SDP member and leader of the rail workers' union. Kun stood for the unamended 1919 policies of the Hungarian leadership, Landler for a more careful reconstruction of the CP using both legal and underground methods.

These forces ultimately decided the outcome of the debate over *History and Class Consciousness*. But, in the first instance, Lukács's work was well received. German revolutionary Karl Korsch's *Marxism and Philosophy* was published the same year and contained an afterword in which Korsch declared himself 'happily in fundamental agreement' with Lukács.[26] Korsch's book did not have the rigour and depth of *History and Class Consciousness*, but it was nevertheless a valuable contribution to re-establishing the 'Hegelian' Marxist tradition and a devastating critique of the fatalism of Second International Marxism. A fellow member of the Hungarian CP leadership, Jozef Revai, also published an intelligent and favourable review of Lukács's book. Revai at least understood the fundamentals of the argument that Lukács was making and the first half of his review is a powerful advocacy of this point of view. But Revai also interpreted Lukács in an idealist framework and exaggerated some of the ambiguous formulations in *History and Class Consciousness*.[27] Lukács later recalled that 'there was only one critic who objected to *History and Class Consciousness* on the grounds that it was insufficiently radical – and that was Revai'.[28] German Communist playwright and critic Karl Wittfogel and Lukács's disciple Bela Forgarasi were among others who welcomed *History and Class Consciousness*.[29] These favourable responses were, however, only a prelude to a much more ominous reception.

In the approach to the Communist International Congress, Hermann Duncker, a leading figure in the Thuringian section of the German CP who had already polemicised against Karl Korsch, published the first critical review of *History and Class Consciousness* in May 1923. Bela Kun, now resident in Moscow, attacked Lukács in a short review of *History and Class Consciousness* which concluded that Lukács's approach was alien to Marxism. By the time of the Congress, *Pravda* was attacking Lukács, Korsch, Revai and Forgarasi as in need of education in the fundamentals of Marxism.[30] But the two most sustained attacks on Lukács came from Lazslo Rudas and Abram Deborin. Rudas was an associate of Lukács before the revolution and had worked with Lukács in exile on the journal *Kommunismus*. Rudas had been part of the opposition to Kun in the HCP. But he had left Vienna for Moscow in 1923, become Kun's secretary and a supporter of the Hungarian leadership. Russian philosopher Abram Deborin was a former Menshevik who was involved in his own bureaucratic struggle for ascendancy in the nascent Soviet academy.

Deborin's contribution to the debate, 'Lukács and his Critique of Marxism', is mainly interesting because it shows how little changed were the fundamental features of Second International Marxism in the minds of some of those who joined the Russian Revolution.[31] Deborin's article ignores the vast majority of Lukács's book. It simply does not discuss the central article 'Reification and the Consciousness of the Proletariat', nor does it engage with Lukács's chapters concerning the revolutionary party. Deborin's almost exclusive focus is on the remarks that Lukács makes about the dialectic of nature and Engels's approach to this issue.

History and Class Consciousness was concerned to warn against the importation of ways of thinking that were appropriate in the natural sciences into Marxist accounts of the class struggle. Lukács saw that such approaches underlay the determinism of Second International Marxism. Some passages of *History and Class Consciousness* can therefore be read as rejecting the view that Marx's method can be applied to both the social and the natural world. There are, however, other passages in *History and Class Consciousness* where Lukács seems to be making a different point. On these occasions, Lukács argues that there is a dialectic in both nature and society but that they are different in form because, in the former, human consciousness is not present, whereas, in the latter, it is an important part of explaining social transformations. Lukács also questions whether Engels's identification of experimentation in the natural sciences with political practice was valid. Lukács points out that in experimentation we observe an objective process in which we play no active role, but in political practice the consciousness and activity of human beings are part of the process of change.

Deborin engages with none of the complexity of Lukács's views, nor indeed with the richness of the issues that he discusses. Deborin simply lumps Lukács together with Korsch, Forgarasi and Revai and asserts not only that Lukács is mistaken about the applicability of the dialectic to nature but also that he is 'on a completely idealist footing in relation to social and historical reality'.[32] The Deborin school was formally interested in the dialectic but they took their understanding at least as much from Plekhanov as from Hegel or Marx. This led to some appreciation of the formal structure of the dialectic but no ability to make these abstractions work at the level of concrete analysis. Deborin uses the same method against Lukács, using Plekhanov's views as much as Marx's as a stick to beat Lukács.

In a revealing passage, for instance, Deborin argues that thought and being should be seen as related, but distinct, parts of a dialectical unity. But this perfectly correct general approach then simply gives way to a series of vintage deterministic formulations: 'Marx never argued for the identity of subject and object, of thought and being. That is pure *idealism* . . . Knowledge or thought only reflects being . . .'[33] Lukács's central point in *History and Class Consciousness* was to show that class location did not simply reflect itself immediately in class consciousness, but that the interaction of resistance to and acceptance of the commodity status of labour power produced a contradictory consciousness. In such a situation, renewed stress on political organisation and political consciousness in resolving this contradiction was the practical conclusion. All this is beyond Deborin, who can see only the labour process as the site of practice: 'the one-sidedness of subject and object is overcome . . . *through praxis*. What is the praxis of social being? The labour process . . . *production* is the concrete unity of the whole social and historical process.'[34] Again, this is formally correct but in fact returns to the old Second

International insistence on the inevitable onward march of the productive process as the guarantor of social change, whereas Lukács, without ignoring this dimension, is concerned with political practice and organisation as well.

Laszlo Rudas's long critique appeared in three sections, the first of which was published on the eve of the Fifth Congress of the International. This first essay deals with the same territory covered by Deborin, Lukács's views on the dialectic of nature. After a lengthy attack on Lukács's views, Rudas summarises his own position: 'Marx and Engels accepted that the dialectic is a natural law, and because society itself is nature, has arisen dialectically from nature (which has different laws but not laws of a different type from nature), so the dialectical law applies itself likewise to the whole of reality, to society as much as to nature. It is simply that in the first case it takes on particular forms.'[35] There is no problem with the perfectly reasonable content of this formulation – but there is a problem with the fact that Rudas does not mention that Lukács himself had made precisely this point in *History and Class Consciousness*. Alongside the more ambiguous formulations to which we have already referred, Lukács also speaks of

> the necessity of separating the merely objective dialectics of nature from those of society. For in the dialectics of society the subject is included in the reciprocal relationship in which theory and practice become dialectical with reference to one another . . . if the dialectical method is to be consolidated concretely it is essential that the different types of dialectics should be set out in a concrete fashion . . .[36]

This passage comes from the central essay on 'Reification and the Consciousness of the Proletariat'. It is possible that Rudas missed it because he, like Deborin, concentrates most of his attention on the earlier, less complex essays.

But Rudas does at least go on to look at the central issue of class consciousness, although, again, more through an examination of the earlier essay of this name than through an analysis of Lukács's major new contribution. The target of Rudas's attack is Lukács's notion of 'imputed consciousness'. This term refers to the view that the class interests of workers differs from their consciousness due to the way in which commodity fetishism operates. This prevents their interests being directly reflected in their consciousness. Lukács argued that it was, nevertheless, possible to 'impute' the consciousness of a class that is able to overcome the effects of commodity fetishism and so become aware of its interests. This notion struck Rudas as nonsensical, an attempt to foist the views of the philosopher on to the working class with no empirical evidence to support such imputation.

Yet a moment's thought reveals that Lukács was not engaged in a particularly unusual theoretical enterprise. In everyday life we often accept that there is a gap between an individual's consciousness and their 'true' interests. We assume that, for some reason, drunk drivers are not acting in their 'real' interests. Many of us accept that praying for the recovery of a sick friend is a form of consciousness that does not correspond to the reality of medical science, or that avoiding walking under ladders betrays a consciousness that does not accurately reflect reality. In all these cases we are happy to assert that if the individuals concerned 'thought about it for a while', or 'stood back and gave it some consideration', they might well not drink and drive, or pray or worry about walking under ladders. We 'impute' a consciousness to them based on an appreciation of what we think they would see their interests to be if they were to look at their situation in a wider framework. Lukács believed that alienation and commodity fetishism constantly induce a state of 'false consciousness', but that the struggle over the control of labour power acts to break down this false consciousness and provide a path by which workers' interests and their ideas could begin to align with each other.

Rudas rejected this approach. He insisted that:

> *The consciousness of humans is a product of the world that surrounds them* . . . This elementary truth is however incompatible with any 'imputation' . . . there is no other hypothetical consciousness, which exists nowhere but in the head of the philosopher, and that can be won after theory has determined the objective historical situation . . . All those who adopt the same position in the process of production have more or less essentially the same consciousness, a class consciousness.[37]

Again, in a deterministic formulation that would have made Kautsky blush, Rudas insists: 'Contemporary society divides into classes. Each class adopts a particular place in the process of production. Each class has different interests . . . In line with their conditions of production and in line with their self-interest, they have a different consciousness. That is precisely what is known as class consciousness!'[38]

If this were true it would be impossible for two workers from the same workplace to hold contradictory ideas, for one to be a Marxist and the other a supporter of a conservative party, for instance. But Rudas simply sweeps this objection aside:

> since the proletariat consists of people . . . who possess consciousness, so they will become aware of their historical mission in time. How do I know that? . . . I know as a materialist that consciousness depends on social being. Since this being is constituted such that the proletariat through its suffering etc. is absolutely of necessity forced into action, so too it is absolutely necessary that in time its consciousness will awaken.[39]

In line with this logic, Rudas does not seem to think that ideological and political battles are necessary to decide whether society progresses or regresses. 'Each stage of the productive forces that is achieved pushes society in a certain direction,' he writes.

> This direction is 'higher' or 'lower', 'progression' or 'regression' depending on circumstances . . . If it is 'progression' then it appears in consciousness as a task that one strives after, and that will in the end be accomplished (providing no interfering factors come into play). If the direction is 'regression', then one can try to arrest it. That might be successful – perhaps, mostly not.[40]

Clearly, there is little room here for explaining how workers can hold competing and contradictory ideas in their minds, or to explain what kind of arguments and organisation might help to resolve such contradictions in a progressive rather than a regressive direction. Human action may be able to effect social change at the margins, but, for the most part, it is strait-jacketed by the productive forces. The methodological

counterpart of this historical determinism was an almost total commitment to a positivist approach.

> Just as in the natural sciences, so in the Marxist science of society, causal-
> ity (or mutual interaction) is a natural or social force that is effective in
> reality. It brings phenomena into certain relationships with each other,
> and this relationship is *given* in reality, *is not alterable*, and our task can only
> consist in seeking out this relationship empirically . . . *What* is cause and
> *what* is effect in a complex of social events is never questionable in
> Marxism . . . *the law bound sequence of the connection of events is not in doubt*.[41]

The long shadow of Second International determinism is clearly visible
in such formulations.

The political consequences of this approach are evident in Rudas's
'Comrade Trotsky on the Proletarian Revolution in Hungary', to which
Lukács replies in this work. Rudas's article is an attack on Trotsky's
Lessons of October. In particular, Rudas is keen to refute Trotsky's claim
that the main reason for the failure of the revolution was the weakness
of the Communist Party. 'No communist can or would say that the only
reason for the fall of the Hungarian Revolution was the missing party
and its merging with the social democratic party,' writes Rudas; 'I do not
want to belittle the importance of the party, but it is a very single minded
approach if you don't take into account all the other factors.' These
other factors include the international military situation, the size of
Hungary which meant that the Red Army could not retreat into the
interior as the Russian Red Army had done, and the inexperience of
Red Army commanders. Rudas concludes his criticism of Trotsky by
insisting that 'the proletarian revolution is a much too complex phenomenon to be reduced to a formula'. And he explicitly links this point
to an attack on 'the newest "orthodox-Marxist" school in Germany (led
by comrade Lukács)' which 'believes that the "only" missing link for the
revolution of the proletariat is the consciousness of the proletariat'.[42]

In Rudas's mind, Trotsky and Lukács are linked because they both
stress the importance of the subjective factor in the revolution. Rudas
steps forth as a defender of the 'objective conditions' which guaranteed
that the revolution was bound to fail. The striking similarity with Karl

Kautsky's review of Korsch's *Marxism and Philosophy*, in which he attributes the failure of the German revolution to just such objective conditions, is striking testimony to the persistence of vulgar Marxism among the emerging Stalinist bureaucracy.[43]

Rudas's response to *History and Class Consciousness* cannot have been a surprise to Lukács. His point of departure in writing *History and Class Consciousness* was that Second International Marxism had grievously distorted the revolutionary essence of Marxism, replacing its dialectical approach with reductionism and determinism, thus undermining the central role played by political organisation and class consciousness in working-class struggle. Rudas's reply was a negative proof that Lukács's diagnosis was correct.

Being right, however, was not enough. If Trotsky's Left Opposition could be bureaucratically silenced in the Russian party, Lukács stood little chance of surviving the wrath of Stalin's followers on the international scene. Zinoviev and Kun used the same methods of manoeuvre, slander and denunciation to isolate Lukács and Korsch. During his opening address to the Communist International's Fifth Congress, Zinoviev vented his spleen on the 'international phenomenon' of 'theoretical revisionism':

> This theoretical revisionism cannot be allowed to pass with impunity. Neither will we tolerate our Hungarian Comrade Lukács doing the same thing in the domain of philosophy and sociology. I have received a letter from Comrade Rudas, one of the leaders of this faction. He says that he had intended to oppose Lukács, but the faction forbade him to do so; thereupon he left the faction because he could not see Marxism watered down. Well done, Rudas! We have a similar tendency in the German party. Comrade Graziadei is a professor. Korsch is also a professor. (Interruption from the floor: 'Lukács is a professor, too!'). If we get a few more of these professors spinning their Marxist theories we shall be lost. We cannot tolerate such theoretical revisionism in our Communist International.[44]

But despite this anti-intellectual thuggery, Lukács continued to defend *History and Class Consciousness*.

Lukács's defence of *History and Class Consciousness*

All the fundamental themes of *History and Class Consciousness* were force-fully restated in Lukács's *Lenin: A Study in the Unity of his Thought*. Lenin died on 21 January 1924 following a nine-month absence from politics. Lukács completed his book the following month. Some commentators have seen *Lenin* as a partial compromise with the bureaucratic trends in the Communist International, an implicit attempt by Lukács to distance himself from the themes of *History and Class Consciousness* by producing an 'orthodox' praise of Lenin.[45] The truth is, however, that *History and Class Consciousness* was itself a Leninist text and that *Lenin* is of a piece with Lukács's concerns in that work, especially the essay 'Towards a Methodology of the Problem of Political Organisation'. Indeed, it is this essay that, in the new text reproduced here, Lukács describes as 'the crucial essay in my book'.[46] It will now be obvious from the new text that this interpretation is correct, but it is also worth noting that the more strictly philosophical innovations of *History and Class Consciousness* are also defended in *Lenin*.

Lukács's basic definition of the dialectic, for instance, remains the same in both works. His concept of totality as the crucial ideological category necessary to overcome the atomising tendencies of capitalist society, of mediation as vital in explaining the links between the appearance of events and their underlying nature, and the essential role played by contradiction in explaining historical change – all these are preserved and expressed concretely in his account of Lenin's thought. The charges of hostility towards the dialectic that he makes against the revisionists of the Second International in *Lenin* are repeated in *Tailism and the Dialectic* in opposition to Rudas. In *Lenin* Lukács makes a point that could easily have been made in *History and Class Consciousness*:

> The Revisionist . . . condemns the dialectic. For the dialectic is no more than the conceptual expression of the fact that the development of society is in reality contradictory, and that these contradictions (class contradictions, the antagonistic character of their economic existence, etc.) are the basis and kernel of all events; for in so far as society is built on class divisions, the idea of 'unity' can only be abstract – a perpetual

transitory result of the interaction of these contradictions. But because the dialectic as a method is only the theoretical formulation of the fact that society develops by a process of contradictions . . . in other words in a revolutionary fashion, theoretical rejection of it necessarily means an essential break with the whole revolutionary standpoint.[47]

All these themes are once again revisited in *Tailism and the Dialectic*. Lukács's reply to Rudas and Deborin makes an unequivocal case for seeing a fundamental unity between *History and Class Consciousness*, *Lenin* and *Tailism and the Dialectic*. It is not necessary to pre-empt Lukács's themes here – his writing speaks clearly enough for itself. But it is perhaps worth noting how the major themes of *Tailism and the Dialectic* will alter some critical judgements about *History and Class Consciousness*.

First, it will make it difficult to sustain the almost universal belief that Lukács inaugurated one of the fundamental traits of 'Western Marxism' – the separation of political organisation from wider issues of social analysis such as alienation and commodity fetishism. In *Tailism and the Dialectic* Lukács makes it absolutely plain that one of the central concerns of his study of the dialectical method and of commodity fetishism is to show that Lenin's theory of the party is their natural consequence. The very first paragraph of *Tailism and the Dialectic* insists that the purpose of *History and Class Consciousness* was 'to demonstrate *methodologically* that the organisation and tactics of Bolshevism are the only possible consequence of Marxism; to prove that, of necessity, the problems of Bolshevism follow logically – that is to say logically in a dialectical sense – from the method of materialist dialectics . . .'.[48] He taxes Rudas with being unable to understand that 'my whole book is concerned with' '*the role of the party in the revolution*'.[49]

Second, it will now be more difficult to claim that *History and Class Consciousness* should be seen as part of Lukács's early ultra-left or 'romantic anti-capitalist' phase. Neither will it be easy to assert that the Heidelberg neo-Kantians continued significantly to influence the arguments of *History and Class Consciousness*. These are charges that were first made against Lukács by Rudas and others in the mid-1920s, although they have often been repeated since. Some of them, especially the link with his early revolutionary ultra-leftism, have been given additional weight by the fact that Lukács was willing to endorse them himself after his capitulation to Stalinism in the late 1920s. The 1967 preface to *History and Class Consciousness* contains comments in this vein. The very least that will now have to be granted is that Lukács did not see it this way in the mid-1920s. Describing such remarks as 'the sauce that Comrade Rudas serves with his tailist cabbage', Lukács continues: 'he knows very well that I have broken with my past completely, not only socially but also philosophically, that I consider what I wrote before my entry into the HCP to be mistaken and wrong in every way'. He also points out that this 'in no way means that I hold everything I have written since 1918 to be correct today'. Indeed, he insists that 'The selection that I made in 1922 in the edition of *History and Class Consciousness* is also a criticism of earlier writings.' These remarks are a powerful vindication of the view that Lukács made a fundamental break with his philosophical past under the impact of the experience of the Russian and Hungarian revolutions. It is also evidence in favour of the case, first made by Michael Löwy, that *History and Class Consciousness* was reconstructed by Lukács as a critique of his own earlier ultra-leftism.[50]

Third, Lukács uses *Tailism and the Dialectic* to defend his conception of 'imputed consciousness', one of the central and most contentious notions of *History and Class Consciousness*. It was the fundamental contention of Althusserian criticisms of *History and Class Consciousness*, most famously that of Gareth Stedman Jones, that Lukács's analysis left no room for working-class struggle in the formation of class consciousness, or for the role of various social institutions in the formation of ideology. Nor did Lukács provide an 'epistemological basis for the role of the party'. These weaknesses left him dependent on a 'catastrophist' notion of economic crises to account for the transformation of false consciousness into revolutionary consciousness.[51] The great virtue of Lukács's defence of imputed consciousness is that it is attached so securely to his basic method on the one hand and to the role of the party on the other that many of these objections are overcome.

Lukács begins by asserting the centrality of the problem as he posed it in *History and Class Consciousness*: 'the proletariat *can* have a correct knowledge of the historical process . . . in accordance with its class position. But does it always have this knowledge? Not at all. And inasmuch as this distance is acknowledged to be a *fact*, it is the duty of every Marxist to seriously reflect on its *causes* . . .'[52] Lukács sees these causes in the commodity structure of capitalist society. These ensure that 'the actual make-up of social phenomena is *not immediately* apparent'.[53] The conflict created by the contradictory nature of capitalist society begins to reveal the real totality of society beyond the alienated and atomised appearance. But this process of coming to consciousness cannot be completed unless that section of the class that has already, on the basis of previous experience and the theoretical generalisation of that experience, become conscious, intervenes to aid others to combat false consciousness.

To reject this notion of false consciousness and how it can be overcome, especially if one does so in the name of a theory that assumes that consciousness simply reflects class position, is a recipe for passivity. Strategically it leads revolutionaries into 'tail-ending' the consciousness of the class. When Rudas insists that Lukács is a subjectivist and an idealist, that he pays too little attention to the objective preconditions of revolution, he forgets that 'the Hungarian proletarian revolution of 1919 failed first and foremost because of the absence of this subjective moment, the Communist Party'.[54] The consequence of such an approach is that 'objective factors', the backwardness of the working class, the proportion of the population who are peasants and so on, are dragged in to account for failures which then appear inevitable but were in fact avoidable.

There is a more general problem with this approach, argues Lukács, because it systematically fails to see how the objective situation and the subjective activity of the class and the revolutionary party are dialectically related. This does not only apply in revolutionary situations. Lukács quotes the theses of the Third Congress of the Communist International to the effect that 'there is no moment when the Communist Party cannot be active'. He explains that this is so 'because there can be no moment where this character of this process, the germ, the possibility of an *active* influencing of the subjective moments is completely lacking'.[55] There is no linear progress to socialism as both Kautsky and Rudas believe:

Development does not occur, then, as a continuous intensification, in which development is favourable to the proletariat, and the day after tomorrow the situation *must* be even more favourable than it is tomorrow, and so on. It means rather that at a *particular* point, the situation demands that a decision be taken and the day after tomorrow might be too late to make that decision.[56]

Subjective and objective constantly trade places. Our wrong subjective decision today will reappear as an objective determinant of our action tomorrow. The objective process and such moments of decision are like a knotted rope; each knot of decision forms part of the objective structure of events stretching out behind us, determining what and how we can decide today. 'It is impossible to separate the "moment" from the "process". The subject does not face the object inflexibly and unconnectedly. The dialectical method does not intend either an undifferentiated unity or a definite separation of moments.'[57]

This notion of 'differentiated unity' lies behind the penultimate issue over which *Tailism and the Dialectic* will overturn some critical judgements. It has often been argued that Lukács rejected the dialectic of nature. These accusations receive their first formulation with Rudas and Deborin. *History and Class Consciousness* provided contradictory evidence on this point, as we have seen. But, in *Tailism and the Dialectic*, Lukács is adamant that he had no intention of rejecting the dialectic of nature. His remarks are unambiguous: 'Self-evidently society arose *from* nature. Self-evidently nature and its laws existed *before* society (that is to say before humans). Self-evidently the dialectic *could* not possibly be effective as an *objective principle of development* of society, if it were not already effective as a principle of development of nature before society, if it did not *objectively exist*.' But Lukács is keen that we see not only the unity between society and nature but also the differentiation between them. 'From that, however, follows neither that social development could produce no new, equally objective forms of movement, dialectical moments, nor that the dialectical moments in the development of nature would be *knowable* without the mediation of these new social dialectical forms.'[58] His further investigation of the relationship between our objective knowledge of nature and the social form in which this knowledge can only be available to us is one of the most interesting passages in *Tailism and the Dialectic*.

It is this distinction between our knowledge of objective nature and nature itself that informs Lukács's discussion of Engels's views on experiment and industry. Engels had made the point that, once we experiment on nature, we come to know it in a way that abolishes its objectivity. In Hegel's terminology, it ceases to be something 'in-itself' and becomes something 'for-us'. Engels went on to argue that this could refute the Kantian doctrine that there was an unbridgeable gap between the thing-in-itself and our knowledge of it. Lukács's objection to this line of argument is that this process is not the same as the one by which the working class becomes *self-conscious*. As Lukács explains it, a thing-in-itself and a thing-for-us are not antonyms but synonyms. They are two sides of the same coin. The opposite of a thing-in-itself is not a thing-for-us, but a thing-for-itself, a thing that has gained self-consciousness. This is the use to which Marx puts these terms when he talks of a class that is merely united by its common economic circumstances as a class in-itself, as opposed to a class that is conscious of its circumstances as a class for-itself. For a natural object to become for-itself it would have to become self-conscious, which is the one thing it cannot do.

Lukács is not trying to deny the power of experiment, nor to deny the reality of the knowledge that results. He is merely trying to insist that experiment alone cannot refute Kantianism, or any other form of bourgeois philosophy. If this were the case, natural scientists would be spontaneous dialectical materialists under the impact of their professional work.

But in reality this is not the case, as is well known. Since for Friedrich Engels the problem of the thing-in-itself is solved and dealt with by historical materialism, *for him* the experiment could *indeed* represent an example of the dialectical conception of reality. For the experimenter, however – if he does not happen to be a disciple of historical materialism – it does not go without saying. For the experiment in which the thing-in-itself becomes a thing-for-us is only in-itself dialectical. In order to reveal its *dialectical* character *for-us*, something else has to come along, something new – precisely historical materialism. Researchers into nature can carry out as many and as marvellous experiments as they like, and still, in spite of it all, cling on to the undiscernibility of the thing-in-itself, or be a Machist, or even Schopenhauerian.[59]

Thus Lukács hopes to preserve the proper relation between what has to be proven by historical materialism and what can be proven by an experimental method which lacks this philosophical framework. He insists that in his general approach Engels did just this, but his would-be disciples have made use of a misformulation to justify their own positivist approach. The dispute is important, but, even if Lukács were mistaken, it hardly marks the break with materialism that Rudas and Deborin allege.

Seen in context, *Tailism and the Dialectic* is Lukács's last great affirmation of the formidable theoretical unity that he forged in *History and Class Consciousness* between a fully effective account of ideology and Lenin's theory of the party. In so doing, he refurbished the Marxist dialectic in a way that has few equals in the twentieth century. Lukács himself, however, was unable to defend his achievement much beyond the composition of *Tailism and the Dialectic*. By 1930 he had become a supporter of Stalin. Through this process Lukács joined those who did more than destroy the Bolshevik party that made the 1917 revolution. They also effectively corrupted the theory of the party that was based on that experience and which Lukács had done so much to elaborate.

Lukács and Stalinism

Why did Lukács become a Stalinist? The story of Lukács's break with revolutionary Marxism is at least as complex as the story of how he became a Marxist in the first place. No full account is possible here. Nevertheless, the fate of *History and Class Consciousness* would not be comprehensible without at least an outline of the circumstances in which this transformation took place.

The fundamental context is constituted by the conditions of the international class struggle from the mid-1920s onwards. Just as the rise of the revolutionary wave drew Lukács into the movement, so the ebb carried him away towards the Stalinist counter-revolution. The period that followed the defeat of the German October in 1923 was an unremitting series of reverses: in Italy, Mussolini tightened his grip on power in the mid-1920s, the British General Strike was defeated in 1926 and the Chinese Revolution crushed in 1927. In Russia, the Stalinist bureaucracy's programme of 'socialism in one country' seemed more plausible with every defeat. And, with every increase in the bureaucracy's strength, it played a more disastrous role in each subsequent revolutionary opportunity.

Lukács had, of course, directly experienced the defeat of the Hungarian Workers' Republic in 1919. His initial reflections on this revolution and his first full encounter with Lenin's work led to *History and Class Consciousness*. But the task of rebuilding the Hungarian CP under Horthy's dictatorship took Lukács in a different direction. As we have seen, Bela Kun learnt nothing and forgot nothing about the policy of the HCP in 1919. His faction remained on its ultra-left course, sustained by Zinoviev. Landler and Lukács tried to rebuild the HCP with a mixture of legal and illegal tactics and it was Landler's faction that controlled the actual reconstruction of the party inside Hungary. By the late 1920s, Lukács was beginning to generalise from this experience. In 1928, the year of Landler's death, Lukács wrote the 'Blum Theses', taking their title from Lukács's party name. Going far beyond the tactical consider-ations of working under the dictatorship, they advocated the wholesale abandonment of the strategy of proletarian revolution and instead called for the HCP to work merely for the dictatorship of the proletariat and the peasantry, that is, merely for a democratic revolution.

In many ways, this foreshadowed the Popular Front strategy that Stalin was to adopt in the 1930s. But Lukács found himself a 'premature Popular Frontist' because, in 1928, the Communist International adopted its ultra-left Third Period perspective in which even social democrats were said to be no different to fascists. Clearly, Lukács's perspective was highly vulnerable to critique by Bela Kun and he lost the argument in the Hungarian CP.

Once more, Lukács found himself at an impasse. The possibility of becoming a revolutionary critic of Stalinism by joining Trotsky's Left Opposition was excluded by Lukács's own rightward evolution. Lukács may also have been influenced by the fact that, when Trotsky relaunched the opposition to Stalin in 1926, he did so in alliance with Zinoviev. Many of Trotsky's own supporters had understandable reservations

about this alliance and it may be that Lukács, so recently the target of
Zinoviev's invective, felt the same. However this may be, Lukács made
his choice. But Lukács immediately found his own perspectives rejected.
He decided to withdraw from active politics and to cultivate philosophical and aesthetic concerns.

Tailism and the Dialectic was followed quickly by an essay on a leading
figure among the Young Hegelians of the 1840s, 'Moses Hess and the
Problems of Idealist Dialectics'.[60] Here, for the first time in Lukács's
thought, there are indications of his collapse into an accommodation
with existing reality. The notion so marked in *Tailism and the Dialectic*, of
the collective action that is possible in any given situation in order to be
able to change that situation, is diminished. Instead, Lukács discovers
a new respect for the later Hegel's 'reconciliation with reality', the
quietude that becomes full-blown in following years.

There is an important methodological point at issue here as well. In
retrospect, Lukács in part attributed his change of perspective to his
reading of Marx's *Economic and Philosophical Manuscripts* in Moscow in
1930 where they were made available for the first time. In his 1967
preface to *History and Class Consciousness*, Lukács makes great play of the
'shock effect' that reading this work had on him. The discovery that
labour is the central way in which humans objectify themselves in the
world and that 'objectification is a natural means by which man masters
the world . . . completely shattered the theoretical foundations of . . .
History and Class Consciousness'. Consequently, Lukács argues, 'the book
became wholly alien to me'.[61]

There are a number of problems with this account. First, *History and
Class Consciousness* had not in fact treated all objectification, that is
all products of human mental and manual labour, as if they were
negative products of alienation. This had been Hegel's error and it is
unlikely that Lukács would simply have reproduced it. Indeed, the text
of *History and Class Consciousness* shows that, while Lukács did not make
a terminological distinction between alienation and objectification, he
did reproduce the distinction, using objectification in both a positive and
a negative sense.[62]

So why did Lukács make so much of labour as the origin of the
Marxist relationship between the subjective and the objective aspects of

reality? A clue is to be found in a point made by Jorge Larrain: 'It may be true that labour is the original form and model of praxis, but without further qualification this formulation risks reducing praxis to labour and probably shows the impact of the official Marxist orthodoxy on the later Lukács.'[63] And, for Lukács in 1930, having just renounced active politics in favour of scholarly seclusion in Moscow's Marx–Engels Institute, there was every reason to remove practice from the political arena and relocate it in the realm of labour. Necessarily, this broke the central hinge on which *History and Class Consciousness* turned – the relationship between consciousness and political organisation. This is not to say that there was no genuine theoretical deepening involved in Lukács's reading of the *Economic and Philosophical Manuscripts*. There was, and the evidence is there to see in Lukács's treatment of economic themes in his *The Young Hegel*. But this deepening did not require the abandonment of *History and Class Consciousness*. In choosing to do so, Lukács lost much more than he gained.

The 'Blum Theses', however, were the real turning point. The reaction to reading the *Economic and Philosophical Manuscripts* reinforced and excused intellectual developments that were already in train. Thereafter, Lukács was often a critic of Stalinism, but only ever a right critic. He consistently pursued an argument in regard to politics, art and philosophy that stressed what the great bourgeois tradition stretching back to the Enlightenment had in common with the Marxist tradition and systematically denied what separated them. Just as consistently, he was hostile to the Trotskyist tradition until the end of his life, even when, in his last years, his old revolutionary ardour began to glow in the fire of the world-wide revolt of 1968 and the years that followed.

It is the great radicalising impulse of those years that lies behind the modern recovery of the full meaning of *History and Class Consciousness*. The crisis in the system that began then has not yet been resolved, even if the level of resistance engendered by it has varied over the intervening years. So long as that crisis continues, those who want to resist its ravages will find sure guidance in *History and Class Consciousness* and *Lenin*. They now also have a valuable defence against criticisms first made in the mid-1920s but which are still heard today.

Notes

I am grateful to Sebastian Budgen for locating materials and to Esther Leslie and Ruth Pallesen-Mustikay for translating documents.

1. The first publication of the original German text and a Hungarian translation was in 1996 by the Budapest journal *Magyar Filozófiai Szemle*.

2. G. Lukács, *Record of a Life* (Verso, 1983), p. 35.

3. Ibid., pp. 37–9.

4. Ibid., p. 43.

5. R. Livingstone, Introduction to G. Lukács, *Tactics and Ethics: Political Writings 1919–1929* (New Left Books, 1972), p. x.

6. Ibid., p. xi.

7. Lukács, *Record of a Life*, p. 43.

8. G. Lukács, 'Preface to the New Edition (1967)', *History and Class Consciousness* (Merlin, 1971), p. xi.

9. I. Mészáros, *Beyond Capital* (Merlin Press, 1995), p. 296.

10. R.L. Tokes, *Bela Kun and the Hungarian Soviet Republic* (London, 1967), p. 87.

11. Quoted in ibid., pp. 133–4.

12. See F.L. Carsten, *Revolution in Central Europe 1918–1919* (Wildwood House, 1988), p. 242.

13. Ibid., p. 241.

14. Ibid., p. 234.

15. Ibid., pp. 245–6.

16. Quoted in L. Congdon, *The Young Lukács* (University of North Carolina Press, 1983), p. 139.

17. It is only in a general sense that it is accurate to describe Lukács's political positions at this time as 'ultra-left'. On a minority of issues, like the cultural policy of the Hungarian Workers' Republic for which Lukács was responsible as Deputy Commissar for Education, he conducted a policy similar to that of Lunacharsky, Trotsky and Lenin in Russia. On certain other crucial issues – like the merger of the HCP with the reformist SDP at the outset of the Workers' Republic – Lukács adopted a 'liquidationist' stand, an error usually regarded as a rightist position. This kind of polarity is common with those who begin with ultra-left attitudes. The gap between their principles and the political reality that they face cannot be bridged on the basis of such abstractions and so, having found no practical lever within the current situation that can be used to change it, they collapse into acceptance of existing reality. The pattern is an old one: Hegel's abstract idealist principles eventually led him into just such a 'reconciliation' with reality.

18. See Lukács, *Tactics and Ethics*, pp. 53–63.

19. M. Löwy, *Georg Lukács – From Romanticism to Bolshevism* (New Left Books, 1979), ch. 4, especially pp. 173–6.

20. Lukács, *History and Class Consciousness*, p. 22.

21. Ibid., p. 178.

22. Ibid., p. 322.

23. Ibid., p. 327.

24. V. Serge, *Memoirs of a Revolutionary 1901–1914* (Oxford University Press, 1980), p. 187.

25. Ibid., pp. 136, 177.

26. See F. Halliday, 'Karl Korsch: An Introduction', in K. Korsch, *Marxism and Philosophy* (New Left Books, 1970), pp. 13–14.

27. J. Revai, 'A Review of Georg Lukács' *History and Class Consciousness*' appeared in *Archiv für die Geschichte des Sozialismus und der Arbeiterbewegung* II (1923), pp. 227–36.

28. Lukács, *Record of a Life*, p. 79.

29. See the useful account of the Lukács debate in A. Arato and P. Breines, *The Young Lukács and the Origins of Western Marxism* (Pluto Press, 1979), pp. 170–82.

30. Ibid., pp. 178–9.

31. A. Deborin, 'Lukács and his Critique of Marxism' originally appeared in *Arbeiterliteratur* (1924). I am grateful to Esther Leslie for the English translation of this text.

32. Ibid., p. 4.

33. Ibid., pp. 17–18.

34. Ibid., p. 29.

35. Rudas's review of *History and Class Consciousness* is to be found in L. Rudas, 'Orthodox Marxism?', *Arbeiterliteratur* IX (1924), pp. 493–517 and 'Lukács' Theory of Class Consciousness', *Arbeiterliteratur* X (1924), pp. 669–97, and *Arbeiterliteratur* XI (1924), pp. 1064–89. This quotation comes from part I, p. 16.

36. Lukács, *History and Class Consciousness*, p. 207.

37. Rudas, part II, pp. 21–3.

38. Ibid., p. 27.

39. Ibid., p. 35.

40. Ibid., p. 16.

41. Ibid., pp. 6–7.

42. L. Rudas, 'Genosse Trotzki über die ungarische Proletarierrevolution', *Internationale Presse-Korrespondenz* 162, pp. 2223–4.

43. K. Kautsky, review of Korsch, *Marxism and Philosophy*, in *Die Gesellschaft* (1924).

44. Quoted in A. Arato and P. Breines, *The Young Lukács*, p. 180.

45. This is, for instance, one of the weaknesses in Arato and Breines's mostly valuable *The Young Lukács*.

46. G. Lukács, *Tailism and the Dialectic*, see p. 94 of the main text.

47. G. Lukács, *Lenin: A Study in the Unity of his Thought* (New Left Books, 1977), p. 55.

48. Lukács, *Tailism and the Dialectic*, see below, p. 47. One of the few studies fully to understand the integral nature of the revolutionary party to Lukács's concerns in *History and Class Consciousness* is Stephen Perkins, *Marxism and the Proletariat, a Lukácsian Perspective* (Pluto Press, 1993); see especially ch. 6.

49. Ibid., p. 48.

50. See Löwy, *Georg Lukács*. See also my *Algebra of Revolution, the Dialectic and the Classical Marxist Tradition* (Routledge, 1998), ch. 5.

51. G. Stedman Jones, 'The Marxism of the Early Lukács' in *Western Marxism: A Critical Reader* (New Left Books, 1977), see pp. 38, 39, 44, 47 and 50.

52. Lukács, *Tailism and the Dialectic*, p. 66.

53. Ibid., p. 79.

54. Ibid., p. 51

55. Ibid., p. 62.

56. Ibid., p. 55.

57. Ibid., p. 56.

58. Ibid., p. 102.

59. Ibid., p. 125.

60. See Lukács, *Tactics and Ethics*, pp. 181–227.

61. Lukács, *History and Class Consciousness*, p. xxxvi.

62. For a supporting argument for this interpretation see Rees, *Algebra of Revolution*, pp. 249–51.

63. J. Larrain, 'Lukács' Concept of Ideology' in T. Rockmore (ed.), *Lukács Today, Sovietica* (1988), vol. 51, p. 64.

Introduction to the
Hungarian edition (1996)

László Illés

Here we make available to the interested reader a previously unknown and unpublished study, written in German, by Georg Lukács. The treatment *Chvostismus und Dialektik* was – if one infers from the references cited – probably written in 1925 or 1926, that is, after the Lenin study (1924)[1] and at the same time as the significant reviews of the Lassalle-Edition and Moses Hess's writings.[2] It is striking that Lukács mentions this work in none of his later reminiscences. The study that he describes as lost in the 'preface' to the new edition of *History and Class Consciousness* (1967; 'My Marxist Development: 1918–1930') ('the manuscript has since been lost') is not the same one as *Chvostismus und Dialektik*, since that text – according to his testimony – was written only after he had familiarised himself with Marx's *Economic and Philosophical Manuscripts*. The present text (almost a small book) does not present a 'new beginning'; as a brilliant defence of *History and Class Consciousness* against attacks by László Rudas and Abram Deborin, it is better classified as a type of rearguard attack. The comprehensive collection of documents *A történelem és osztálytudat a huszas évek vitáiban* (*History and Class Consciousness in the Discussions of the 1920s*), compiled by Tamás Krausz and Miklós Mesterházi, in the yearbook of the journal *Filozófiai Figyelö*, Budapest, 1981, vol. I–IV [contributions in original languages] considers the broad array of critical positions on *History and Class Consciousness*. The editors cannot have known then that Lukács undertook this attempt to defend his work. He undertook it in the heightened political atmosphere after the Fifth Congress of the Comintern (June–July 1924), at which Zinoviev's attacks against him 'rang out'. (As is well known, the articles by Rudas and Deborin were published during the build-up to the Congress.)

Later specialist literature that has dealt with this period of Lukács's writing has attempted to free him from the stigma of 'ultra-radicalism'; and he himself in his 'preface' remembers the rethinking of his positions in the run-up to the 'Blum-Theses' (1928–29).[3] The study *Chvostismus und Dialektik* demonstrates, in contrast to this, that in the years 1925–26 Lukács had not rethought his position at all. His increased emphasis on 'imputed consciousness' even goes beyond that in *History and Class Consciousness*, and he continues to maintain his criticism of Engels's dialectic of nature, though not without here formulating the thesis more elastically and in a more nuanced way. The study documents that Lukács did not let himself be pushed into the epochal change to 'après la révolution' of the bureaucratic consolidation after the Fifth Congress, but rather – if 'belatedly' – holds on firmly to the recollection of 'revolutionary messianism'. This newly discovered study represents a significant milestone in the intellectual development of Georg Lukács in the middle of the 1920s.

The discovery of the manuscript came within the framework of a Hungarian–Russian research project, under the direction of the Institute for Literary Science at the Hungarian Academy of Sciences (László Illés) and the Institute of Slavistics and Balkanistics at the Russian Academy of Sciences (W.T. Sereda and A.S. Stikalin). On the Hungarian side, the research project is also supported by the University of Miskolc, the OTKA Foundation and the Lajos Magyar Foundation. The aim of the project is to collect together all the documents that reflect the political and intellectual activity of Georg Lukács in the former Soviet Union. The material sought is all unpublished material by and on Georg Lukács from the 1920s until the final years of the Soviet Empire. It is only now accessible in the various Russian archives.

The typescript that is published here for the first time, whose external description follows in the editor's notes, was discovered in the joint archive of the Comintern and the Central Party Archive of the CPSU (Rossijskij Centr Hranjenija I Isutschenija Dokumentov Nowejsej

Istorii – RCCHIDNI). It bears the shelf mark: Fond. 347, op. 1, delo 188, and it stems from the contents of the former Lenin Institute. Lukács probably sent it from Vienna to there or to another department or editorial team. On the cover page of the typed script there is a pencilled remark in Russian: 'K.F. Inst. Lenina. Destroy maybe? Incomprehensible script from a whinger who does not express his point of view clearly and straightforwardly – 31.10.1941. Podvojskij.' It is possible that this note was made during the wartime evacuation of the Institute from Moscow.

Permission for the first publication of the German original text as well as the Hungarian translation (both in the journal *Magyar Filozofiari Szemle*, Budapest) was granted on 21 February 1996 by the director of the archive, Dr Kiril Mihajlowitsch Anderson, and it is listed under number 187/4.

Editorial notes to the Hungarian–German edition

The typewritten script by Georg Lukács, *Chvotismus und Dialektik*, was found in the RCCHIDNI (Russian Centre for the Preservation and Study of Documents of Recent Times) in Moscow. It is written on large-format carbon copy paper, and is furnished with ink corrections from Lukács's hand. It is ninety-two pages long. The text breaks off on the last available page, but from the logic of the argument one can conclude that probably only a couple of pages are missing.

The text of this first publication is faithful to the original and unexpurgated. In order to facilitate better legibility, abbreviations have been deciphered (d.h., u.z., gen. R or Gen D. = *das heißt, und zwar, Genosse Rudas und Deborin*). Antiquated modes of writing have been updated to present standards (Oekonomie = Ökonomie). Incorrect articles of nouns and wrong declination of adjectives have been corrected. Despite Lukács's handwritten corrections, it appears that several words that should be there according to the sense of a sentence are missing and have not been added by him. The editors have supplemented these in square brackets [. . .]. Words or passages of text in round brackets (. . .) always stem from Lukács himself. Some of these brackets remained unfilled. It is relevant to mention here that Lukács does not always render quotations exactly. Furthermore the Plekhanov article about 'knots' cannot be found at the place cited. The name Duhau, mentioned in the text, is probably a misspelling of Duhem.

Lukács's polemic is predominantly against critical articles by Abram Deborin and László Rudas. Their treatments appeared in the periodical *Arbeiterliteratur* (edited by Johannes Wertheim, Vienna, Verlag für Literatur und Politik, 1924), and Lukács refers to it by the abbreviation A.L. The abbreviation G.u.K, for *Geschichte und Klassenbewußtsein – Studien über marxistische Dialektik* [*History and Class Consciousness: Studies in the Marxist Dialectic*], (Kleine revolutionäre Bibliothek, vol. 9; Berlin, Malik Verlag, 1923) likewise stems from Lukács. Very often he refers to a collected volume, which he reviewed in 1926 in the *Archiv für die Geschichte der Arbeiterbewegung und des Sozialismus* [*Archive for the History of the Labour Movement and Socialism*]. This is V.I. Lenin's *Ausgewählte Werke. Sammelband – Der Kampf um die soziale Revolution* (Vienna, Verlag für Literatur und Politik, 1925). Similarly he often uses as a source *Gegen den Strom* [*Against the Stream*], a collected volume that appeared in 1921 in the imprint of the Communist International, in Hamburg and Petrograd, with contributions from Lenin and Zinoviev, which had previously appeared in the Swiss periodical *Sozial-Democrat*, between the years 1914 and 1917. Lukács published numerous contributions from his 'left-radical' period in the organ *Kommunismus* – the periodical of the Comintern for the countries of Southern Europe (Vienna, 1920–21; edited by Gerhardt Eisler). *Inprekorr*, i.e. *Internationale Pressekorrespondenz*, appeared in Berlin as a bulletin of the Comintern from 24 September 1921 to 1932; subsequently it was known as *Rundschau* and was produced out of Basel.

Several institutions and parties need explanation: VIVA = Vereinigung Internationaler Verlagsanstalten [Union of International Publishing Houses], EKKI stands for Exekutivkomitee der Kommunistischen Internationale; S.R. for the party of Social Revolutionaries, a petty bourgeois tendency, which emerged from the ranks of the Narodniki in 1902 and disputed the leading role of the Bolsheviks and the legitimacy of proletarian dictatorship. And finally tail-ending (from the Russian *khvost* = tail, train, correspondingly tailist politics) was a tendency that was opposed to Bolshevism – it insisted on the spontaneity of the masses, negated the necessity of a Marxist party and denied the significance of class consciousness. Its representatives in the Russian labour movement were the so-called Economists, who were singled out for heavy attack by Lenin in his 1902 book *What is to be Done* – whereby he himself used the term tail-ending.

Lukács's antagonists here are: Abram Moissejevich Deborin (orig. Joffe; 1881–1963), Soviet philosopher, pupil of G.W. Plekhanov, from 1926 to 1930 editor-in-chief of the periodical *Pod snamenem marksisma*; later fell from grace. László Rudas (1885–1950), Hungarian philosopher, founder member of the CP in Hungary, editor of *Vörös Újság* (*Red Flag*); after the fall of the Hungarian council republic he emigrated to the Soviet Union, principal associate of the Institute for Marxism–Leninism; lecturer at the so-called 'Red Chair'; after 1945 university professor and member of the Academy in Budapest.

Notes

1. *Lenin: A Study in the Unity of his Thought* (New Left Books, 1970). [Trans.]

2. These both appear in the 1968 edition of collected early writings, which also contained the reissue of *History and Class Consciousness*, and Lukács's new and self-critical preface. *Frühschriften* II, Band 2 der Werkausgabe (Luchterhand, Neuwied, 1968). [Trans.]

3. See, for example, 'Preface to the New Edition' (1967), *History and Class Consciousness* (Merlin Press, 1971), pp. xxvii–xxx. [Trans.]

Translated by Esther Leslie

Tailism and the Dialectic

Georg Lukács

Translated by Esther Leslie

Some critiques of my book *History and Class Consciousness* have appeared (written by Comrades L. Rudas and A. Deborin in issues IX, X and XII of *Arbeiterliteratur*) which I simply cannot let pass without a response. In and of themselves, the harshest criticisms would have been quite welcome. In the introduction to my book (p. xlvi) I characterised it explicitly as a discussion document. There are many things in the book that I deem needful of correction. I would formulate many of the things contained therein quite differently today. It is certainly not my intention *to defend the book itself.* I would be only too glad if I could regard it as completely redundant, if I could see that its purpose had been fully accomplished. What is this purpose? To demonstrate *methodologically* that the organisation and tactics of Bolshevism are the only possible consequence of Marxism; to prove that, of necessity, the problems of Bolshevism follow logically – that is to say logically in a dialectical sense – from the method of materialist dialectics as implemented by its founders. If the discussion of my book had left not one stone standing, but had meant that some progress had been achieved in this respect, I would have silently enjoyed that progress, and not defended one single claim in my book.

But my critics move instead in the *opposite direction*. They use their polemics to smuggle Menshevik elements into Marxism and Leninism. I have to retaliate. I am not defending my book. I am attacking the open Menshevism of Deborin and the tail-ending of Rudas. Deborin sticks to his guns: he was always a Menshevik. Comrade Rudas is, however, a Bolshevik. I know him from many years of communal party work. But precisely because of that I am in no position to reciprocate his acknowledgement ('He never wavered for a minute. He was always an avowed enemy of opportunism', *Arbeiterliteratur* IX, p. 493)[1] with comments on his activity. Questions about the development of the Hungarian Communist Party do not belong in this debate, so instead I will develop Comrade Rudas's – permanently present – inclination towards tail-ending out of his philosophical arguments. And I will draw on only his latest political article, which he wrote 'after a two-year apprenticeship in the Russian CP' ('Comrade Trotsky on the Hungarian Proletarian Revolution', *Inprekorr* IV, p. 162), in order to illustrate his way of seeing. In no way am I complaining, as Comrade Rudas suspects (*Arbeiterliteratur* XII, p. 1080), about 'misunderstandings'.[2] No. I agree with him that 'misunderstandings are not of a logical type'. But precisely because of that I find it completely understandable that he does not understand me: he does not understand *the role of the party in the revolution* and has therefore been *unable* to notice that my whole book is concerned with that question. That is no surprise in the case of the Menshevik Deborin. The opposite would be more surprising.

I. Problems of Class Consciousness

1. Subjectivism

Every time an opportunistic attack is made on the revolutionary dialectic, it proceeds under the banner – against subjectivism. (Bernstein against Marx, Kautsky against Lenin.) Among the many *isms* that Deborin and Rudas attribute to me (idealism, agnosticism, eclecticism, etc.) subjectivism takes pride of place. In the following exposition I will prove that what is at stake is actually always the question of the role of the party in the revolution, and that Deborin and Rudas wage war against Bolshevism when they believe that they are fighting my 'subjectivism'.

First of all, then: what is to be understood by the term 'subject'? And – the next question is inseparable from the first one, indeed its answer allows one to answer the first question correctly – what is the function of the subject in the historical process of development? Rudas and Deborin share, in part, the vulgar standpoint of bourgeois everyday life and its science: inflexibly and mechanistically, they split subject from object. They regard as worthy of scientific investigation only that which is free of any participation on the part of the subject, and they protest in a tone of extreme scientific indignation if an *active and positive* role is accorded to a subjective moment in history. It is only logical then that Deborin assigns to me (*Arbeiterliteratur* X, p. 629) the theory of the identity of thought and being, of subject and object,[3] even though in my book it expressly states that: '. . . their identity is that they are moments of one and the same real historical and dialectical process' (HCC, p. 204). The intentional and unintentional perversion of my thoughts into their opposite becomes understandable if we recall Deborin's own conception of subject and object. He says (p. 639): '. . . that the *sole* [! my italics] materialist sense of this "mutual influence" can only be its conception as a process of labour, as a process of production, as activity, as *the struggle of society with nature*' (my italics).

So, for Deborin, there is *no class struggle*. 'Society struggles with nature' and that is it! What takes place within society is mere appearance, subjectivism. Therefore for him – quite logically – subject = individual and object = nature, or subject – society and object – nature (ibid.). Deborin does not acknowledge that a historical process takes place *inside* society, which alters the relationship between subject and object. To put it mildly, historical materialism is hereby revised and turned into something out of Comte or Herbert Spencer.

Comrade Rudas does not go quite so far. He admits that classes and class struggle exist. Indeed, there are even passages in his writing where he mentions the existence and importance of proletarian activity and the role of the party. But it always remains a formal acknowledgement of the Leninist theory of revolution. In general he quite consistently represents the opposite position. Let us hear it from him himself: 'What is a "historical role"? A role that like every other one, *takes place independently of* – although also through – *human consciousness* of this role' (loc. cit., p. 678, my italics).

Or: 'People have thoughts, feelings. They even set themselves goals –

and they even imagine that these thoughts, these feelings play an important and independent role in history; these aims are the same ones as
those that are accomplished in history' (ibid., pp. 685ff).

The most important thing to note here is that Comrade Rudas speaks
continually of 'history', 'the' person. He 'forgets' – which follows as a
logical consequence of his basic argument – that the issue is not 'the'
person, but the proletariat and its leading party, that it is not history in
general, but the epoch of the proletarian revolution. He 'forgets' that the
crucial point of my formulations, against which he rails, lies in the fact
that the relationship of consciousness and being is ordered differently for
the proletariat than for every previous class that has emerged in society.
The active function of proletarian class consciousness gains a new significance in the epoch of revolution.

This belongs to the ABC of Marxism, and in particular to the ABC
of Leninism. Unfortunately, one is forced to repeat this ABC in the face
of the renewed attempts of Menshevism to turn Marxism into a bourgeois sociology, with formal, trans-historical laws that exclude all 'human
activity'. According to Rudas, characteristic of the historic role is that it
'takes place independently of human consciousness'.

Let us look at how Lenin describes the essence of the historic role:
'The bourgeois regime is going through an extraordinary revolutionary
crisis across the whole world. We must now "prove" through the praxis
of revolutionary parties that they are sufficiently self-conscious to forge
organisations, contacts with the exploited masses, that they possess determination and knowledge to exploit this crisis for the benefit of a
successful, a victorious revolution' ('Speech on the World Situation at the
2nd Congress of the Comintern', *The Second Congress of the Communist
International*, Volume 1 (London, 1977), p. 24). And, after he has
described the objective preconditions of a revolutionary situation,
'which are independent of the will of not only single groups and parties,
but also single classes', he speaks of why, given the presence of such conditions, a revolution is not always bound to break out: 'Because it is not
the case that out of every revolutionary situation a revolution transpires,
but only out of such a situation where, in addition to the objective conditions outlined previously, a subjective factor comes along, namely the
capability of the revolutionary *class* to carry out revolutionary mass

actions that are of sufficient strength to break the old government (or shake it), which never, even in a period of crisis, "collapses" unless one "rattles" it' (*Against the Stream*).

Comrade Rudas does not share this opinion. His 'youthful error' – that the Hungarian proletarian revolution of 1919 failed first and foremost because of the absence of this subjective moment, the Communist Party – is completely withdrawn. Nobody, not even Rudas in his 'subjectivist' period, maintained that it was because of that fact alone that it failed. In the past, as in the present, Rudas shows himself to be a faithful Kantian: whether he over- or underestimates 'the subjective moment', he always carefully *separates* it off from the 'objective' and guards against regarding the two moments in their *dialectical interaction*. Now he wants to show that the Hungarian Dictatorship of Workers' Councils failed because of 'objective' obstacles. As examples of these, he introduces the diminutive size of the territory, which provided no opportunity for a military withdrawal, betrayal on the part of the officers, and the blockade. All three things are facts. All three played an important role in the demise of the Hungarian dictatorship. However – and this *methodological* point of view is decisive for our controversy – if we want to remain revolutionary dialecticians, Leninists, none of these moments can be considered in their mere facticity, independent of the question of whether or not there was a Communist Party. Blockade, hunger! Yes indeed, but Comrade Rudas must admit that the hunger, the lack of commodities, etc., do not come even remotely close to the deprivations of the Russian proletariat, and the standard of living of our workers did not even sink to the level of conditions in Vienna. What was fateful for the Dictatorship of Workers' Councils, in terms of the blockade, was the social-democratic demagogy that insisted that a return to 'democracy' would mean an end to the blockade and the raising of the workers' standard of living. What was fateful was the fact that the workers believed this demagogy – precisely because there was no Communist Party there. Officer betrayal! But Comrade Rudas, as a leading active comrade, must have known that in all places where reasonably capable communists were among the army's ranks, their corps remained reliable and ready to fight until the end. Was it really 'objectively' impossible for our eight divisions (and corresponding regiments, etc.) to find

communist commandants and commissars? It was impossible because
no Communist Party was there to make the choices, carry out the
appointments, and determine the correct course of action. The diminutive size of the territory! Comrade Rudas evokes Trotsky as an authority
for this. If I wanted to be spiteful I would draw from his formulations an
'objective sociological' conclusion: in a small country, a country without
Russia's possibilities of retreat, no dictatorship is possible at all, because
of the imperialist neighbours. (This is, then, the situation of every
European country.) I simply want to remind Rudas that the fall of the
dictatorship was not a purely military affair. On 1 August the Red Army
found itself embarking on a very promising counter-offensive, with some
successes (the recapturing of Szolnok), just as the Workers' Council
Republic stepped down in Budapest, precisely because no Communist
Party existed.

Obviously, the fact that there was no Communist Party in Hungary
during the Dictatorship of Workers' Councils has objective causes.
However, these objective causes were, on the one hand, in part previously subjective ones (sic!) (moments from the history of the workers'
movement). On the other hand, the significance of the subjective
moment is only banished from the world by Kantians who inflexibly
and undialectically separate out subject and object, by making the subject's appearance, the possibility of its effectiveness, the possibility of its
decisive significance, rest on objective causes. In fact the opposite is
true. It is precisely their linkage that demonstrates the dialectical relationship of interaction that I was concerned to address in my book, and
whose existence is – more or less openly – repudiated by Deborin and
Rudas.

Put as a general philosophical statement (that is to say, in this case,
put wrongly) this interaction is meant to indicate that the subjective
mirroring of the objective process is an actual, operative moment of the
process itself, and not only something imagined. Such subjective mirroring does not only form an unavoidable link between any two objective
moments, a link that might be, however, disregarded in an 'objective'
consideration of things, since it is not important for 'objective' analysis.
It also shows that people actually – and not only in their imagination –
make their own history. We said 'put as a general philosophical

statement means, in this case, put wrongly'. Why? Because this state of affairs *comes into being only with the emergence of the proletariat*, because the proletariat is the first, and until now, the *only* subject in the course of history for whom this perception is valid. All thinkers, then, who have ascribed to real or fantastic subjects (great men, national spirits, etc.) such an effect on reality, on the course of history, were necessarily idealist in their method and, in their findings, they could only arrive at false constructions, historical mythologies.

Of course, bourgeois science, and the Menshevism that is completely influenced by it, denies any possibility of influencing reality, even on the part of the proletariat, or it admits it only in a fantastic mythological form. Both cases are underpinned by the same *unhistorical* conception of reality. Just as medieval, feudal ideology forged a trans-temporal relationship between the person and god, so bourgeois and Menshevik ideology constructs a trans-temporal 'sociology'. Hereby the fundamental forms of existence of bourgeois society appear (of course in a more or less distorted ideological form) as forms of existence in the past and the future, as ur-communism and social revolution. In contrast to this, precisely because it is an instrument of its revolutionary practice, it is vital for the proletariat's body of knowledge to liberate itself from this way of seeing. It must discover in reality the concrete role inherited by the proletariat as the subjective factor in history, and it must be clear about the function that its (and *only* its) class consciousness possesses in the historical process.

Comrade Rudas places himself among the ranks of those who deny this possibility and in the process he gets embroiled in the greatest contradictions. With the help of quotations ripped out of context – he makes out that I think that the decisive moment in every class struggle is the capacity of the class *adequately* to grasp the totality of society. But I emphasise quite explicitly in my book that the class that is called upon to rule, and the class that is wavering, doomed to defeat, are distinguished by whether or not from each class point of view 'the totality of the existing society is *not* visible *at all*'[4] (HCC, p. 52), or whether the class possesses the capacity to 'organise the whole of society in accordance with [its] interests' (ibid.). And in respect of this totality, I say that every class has to be looked at in terms of 'an exact study of the point in the total process of production at which the interests of the various classes are most immediately and vitally involved. Secondly, we would have to show how far it would be in the interest of any given class to go beyond this immediacy, to annul and transcend its immediate interest by seeing it as a factor within a totality. And lastly, what is the nature of the totality that is then achieved? How far does it really embrace the true totality of production?' (HCC, p. 54). In this way, it will be possible to distinguish the various forms of 'false consciousness' from each other. On this basis I set out thoroughly (pp. 55–9) how in pre-capitalist societies *every* class can *only* possess 'false consciousness', after the analysis of classes in bourgeois society has attained this *special* sort that has *never* existed before in history (an adequate conception of the social whole) and function (a real and conscious influence on the historical process), in the form of proletarian class consciousness. Ignorant of both the historical grading of questions of class consciousness and the special meaning of these questions in the case of the proletariat, Rudas triumphantly counters my 'idealism' and my 'subjectivism'. I am, of course, completely in agreement with him that misunderstandings are not of a logical type. And so I ask: why did the misunderstanding arise for Rudas, what is its source, and what is its political aim? His conclusions reveal quite clearly the source: his tailist fatalism.

This fatalism appears quite crassly when he directs the harshest of attacks against my so-called 'theory of the moment' (*Arbeiterliteratur* XII, pp. 1077–8).[5] I do not want to dwell once more on his farcical 'misunderstanding', which makes out that I think the role of great personalities is what is at issue. Comrade Rudas 'misunderstands' me here in order not to have to take on board a *fundamental principle* of Bolshevism. Enlisting that tried and trusted tailist trick, he counteracts this theory of the 'blink of an eye', a 'moment' within the process, which I apparently completely neglect (ibid., p. 1082). I am not going to cite the countless passages in my book (e.g. pp. 256–7, 315) where it is blindingly obvious that this is not the case. Comrade Rudas is, however, correct to the extent that he speaks of 'process' in *opposition* to 'moment', for his tailist–fatalist concept of process really does exclude any *moment of decision*. But he makes things too easy for himself, and betrays too clearly his innermost convictions: for him, there are absolutely no moments of decision, his 'process' is an evolution mechanistically and fatally leading from one stage of social development to the next. Of course, this is never put so bluntly. Comrade Rudas (like every tail-ender today) is much too prudent to sever the connection with Lenin, but precisely the way in which he opposes 'process' to 'moment' communicates his view clearly. What is a 'moment'? A situation whose duration may be longer or shorter, but which is distinguished from the process that leads up to it in that it forces together the essential tendencies of that process, and demands that a *decision* be taken over the *future direction of the process*. That is to say the tendencies reach a sort of zenith, and depending on how the situation concerned is handled, the process takes on a different direction after the 'moment'. Development does not occur, then, as a continuous intensification, in which development is favourable to the proletariat, and the day after tomorrow the situation *must* be even more favourable than it is tomorrow, and so on. It means rather that at a *particular* point, the situation demands that a decision be taken and the day after tomorrow might be too late to make that decision. Comrade Rudas might like to think of Lenin's article on 'compromise', where, according to Lenin's view, several days' delay made the offer of compromise with the Mensheviks and the Socialist Revolutionaries (SR's) redundant, and where he notes 'that the days in which peaceful development was possible are already over' ('On Compromises', CW 25, p. 314). Or he might think of Lenin's anxiety that the Bolsheviks might miss the moment when seizure of power would be possible in the October days: 'History would never forgive the revolutionaries if they hesitated when today they could win (and certainly will win), while tomorrow they could lose so much, indeed everything' (CW 26, p. 235).

Of course, Comrade Rudas will deny that his view is contrary to the fundamental conception of Lenin. He prepares the ground for this reproach with noteworthy care: on the one hand, he makes out that the 'moment'[6] stands in contrast to the 'process', as if the process does not arise out of a long sequence of moments, of which, naturally, some tower so much above the others in terms of their quantitative significance that this quantity transforms (cf. Plekhanov on the 'significance of the knotted line of mass conditions', *Neue Zeit* X, I, p. 230); on the other hand, by ascribing to me an idealist subjectivism. And yet I stress – and I do not see the slightest cause to retract any of my reflections or to weaken them in any way – that in such moments everything depends on class consciousness, on the conscious will of the proletariat. This is where the moment of decision lies. The dialectical interaction of subject and object in the historical process consists in the fact that the subjective moment is, self-evidently as I stress again and again, a product, a moment of the objective process. It works back on the process, in certain historical situations, whose emergence is called forth by the objective process (e.g. HCC, p. 313), and gives it direction. This working back is only possible in praxis, only in the *present* (that is why I am using the word 'moment' – in order to highlight this practical and contemporary character). Once the action is completed, the subjective moment slots back into the sequence of objective moments. Thus for each party its own ideological development – Proudhonism in France, Lassalleanism in Germany – is an objective factor, with which each Marxist politician has to reckon as an objective fact. The dialectical interaction that I have outlined above arises 'exclusively' in praxis. In 'the abstract', that is in terms of thought severed from praxis, subject and object clearly do indeed stand cut off from each other, and each thought that ascribes this characteristic of praxis simply to theory ends up in a mythology of concepts, and must become idealist (Fichte). But just as much, all thought – and this is the case with Rudas – that misunderstands this specific character of proletarian praxis, a praxis that is revolutionary, ends up in fatalism, if it carries over the rigid opposition of subject and object from 'pure' theory into praxis. Thereby, it abolishes praxis. It becomes a theory of tail-ending.

It is impossible to separate the 'moment' from the 'process'. The subject does not face the object inflexibly and unconnectedly. The dialectical method does not intend either an undifferentiated unity or a definite separation of moments. On the contrary rather: it invokes an uninterrupted process of moments becoming independent and the uninterrupted abolition of this independence. Just how this dialectical interaction of moments of the process with this reiterated abolition of independence looks is demonstrated repeatedly in my book. Here it is just a matter of understanding that this (dialectical and therefore dialectically overcome) independence of the subjective moment in the contemporary stage of the historical process, in the period of proletarian revolution, is a decisive characteristic of the general situation. It ought to be assumed that this conception is a commonplace – among Leninists. How is it possible even to imagine Lenin's basic idea of the preparation and organisation of revolution without such an *active and conscious* role of the subjective moment? And who could possibly imagine without this function of the subjective moment Lenin's conception of the decisive moments of the revolution – that is the doctrine that stems from Marx but is first made concrete by Lenin – that insurrection is an art? And were not all the reproaches cast against Lenin (even from Rosa Luxemburg) precisely determined by the view that the revolution would come about through economic forces, so to speak 'by itself', that is to say, in other words, 'spontaneously', 'from the base', without the decisive role of *conscious subjective* elements?

In his decisive formulations on insurrection as an art Comrade Lenin first of all distinguishes the Marxist concept of insurrection from the Blanquist one ('Marxism and Insurrection', in *Preparing for Revolt*, also 'Letter to the Comrades'). In the course of this he emphasises how the objective development of the revolution must press on the insurrection (war, starvation, the peasant movement, the wavering of the upper classes, the revolutionary development of the proletariat), in order for the insurrection to be successful, and how this development affects the attitude of the working class. (In July the workers and soldiers 'would not have been willing to *fight* and *die*, for the possession of the town', ibid.) But once the objective situation has ripened to insurrection, once the 'moment' of insurrection is there, then the *conscious, subjective* moment of the revolutionary process raises itself to an independent activity. Lenin contrasts most sharply the merely basal and revolutionary appearance of the masses with this active, decisive intervention of the most class-conscious vanguard. This is what he writes about the situation before autumn and in autumn: 'And, on the other hand, the silent despair of the masses *who feel* that henceforth half-measures will not bring salvation, that it is impossible to "influence" the government, that the starving will "sweep all away, will break down everything anarchically", if the Bolsheviks do not know how to lead them in the decisive struggle'

('Letter to the Comrades', CW 26, p. 210). If we look more closely now at his remarks on insurrection itself, in the passage that invokes 'Revolution and Counter-revolution in Germany', from a methodological point of view, which is the one that concerns us here, we see that they emphasise, on the one hand, moments that are consciously *made*, that is to say brought into being by the subjective side (by the conscious acting subject – grouping of forces, surprise attacks, etc.). And on the other hand, they point most markedly to purely subjective moments (decisiveness, moral superiority, etc.). Insurrection as an art is, then, one moment of the revolutionary process where *the subjective moment has a decisive predominance*. It is superfluous to repeat that the possibility of this predominance, the favourable objective situation for the insurrection, as well as the presence of such a subject, a Communist Party, is a product of social and economic development, though naturally none develops *independently* of the subject, none is a mere product of the basal social process of development. The subjective moment reaches in this 'moment' its comprehensive significance precisely because and inasmuch as it has already acted consciously and actively during earlier developments. (A good counter-example is the German October with Thalheimer as a theorist of spontaneous tail-ending.) But in that 'moment', the decision, and with it the fate of the proletarian revolution (and therefore of humanity), depends on the subjective element. It is impossible to understand correctly the Leninist conception of the revolutionary process without understanding this central significance of insurrection as an art. Lenin said that in the current period (but this relates to *all* revolutionary situations) 'one cannot be faithful to Marxism, to the revolution, *without treating insurrection as an art*' (CW 26, p. 27).

Of course, Lenin turned sharply on any form of 'left' subjectivism (and on one such occasion I received a well-deserved censure from him in respect of an article on parliamentarianism in *Kommunismus* in 1920). However, precisely this clash shows most clearly that Lenin did not fight recognition of the subjective moment on principle, but merely its *incorrect application* – on the one hand, each incorrect estimation of the objective situation; that is to say conceptions that in a overly simplified manner regard the decisive 'moment' as present, when it is objectively not there. And on the other hand, conceptions that mechanically generalise the decisive role ascribed to the actively conscious subjective moment to the whole process, imagining such an influence would be possible at any time and under all conditions and not simply under quite particular concrete conditions. That is to say, then, as is the case with those who – in a back-to-front way, like Comrade Rudas who completely dissolves 'moments' into the 'process', and so (seen in the best light) arrives at a Luxemburgist theory of spontaneity – turn the concrete truth of particular and concrete historical 'moments' into the abstract falsehood of a permanently decisive influenceability of the process. Such a 'left' theory of moments ignores precisely the instant of dialectical change, the concrete, revolutionary essence of the 'moment'. Insurrection as an art is turned into insurrection as a game. The well-warranted active role of the subject turns into an empty phraseology of subjectivism.

But, with the rule of the proletariat, so significant a quantitative shift comes into being that it gains a qualitative character. If the dictatorship of the proletariat is exercised by a real Communist Party (that is to say *not* as it happened in Hungary), this function of the subjective moment acquires a certain consistency, admittedly one that is dialectically restricted. It is not a question of the party arbitrarily changing the economic structure of the country, but rather that in the struggle of the various economic and social tendencies that evidently obtain ever more from the base, the party (and through it just as much the state apparatus as the mass of the workers) is in a position to influence *consciously* and *actively* the development of these tendencies. Lenin, it is true, fiercely contested at every opportunity those 'left' comrades who overestimated the meaning, strength and consistency of this moment, but not as a matter of principle. Rather, because the question they posed was abstract, and because this abstractness distorted the concrete, dialectical moments of the concrete situation. But he fought no less fiercely against those who mistook the significance of the subjective moment, those who capitulated in a defeatist manner before the base, before the tendencies that derive necessarily from the economy. I will simply quote the following sentences from a speech to the Eleventh Party Congress of the RCP: 'State capitalism is the sort of capitalism that we are in a position to limit, whose boundaries we can determine. This capitalism is tied to the state and the state is the workers, the most advanced section of the workers, the vanguard – we are that. State capitalism is the type of capitalism for which we must set certain limits, but we were in no position to set such limits before. That is all. It depends on us how this state capitalism turns out.' ('Political Report of the CC of the RCP(B)', *Speeches at Party Congresses, 1918–22* (Moscow, 1971), p. 306.)

'It depends on us,' Lenin said. Of course not in each and every case, and not always in the same way everywhere. But it is a distortion of Lenin's teachings, a bending of them into tail-ending and Menshevism, to maintain (as Comrade Rudas does – *Arbeiterliteratur* XII, p. 1085), that, according to Lenin, 'an enormous step forward must be taken in developing the productive forces' as necessary prelude to revolution.[7] Just as it is a distortion of my views to claim that 'only' the class consciousness of the proletariat is the driving force of revolution. In *certain situations* (this is why I use the terminology of the moment) it is unquestionably the decisive element. Even Comrade Rudas will admit that in the course of the revolution very favourable moments were not exploited. But it is not Bolshevik, not Leninist, to maintain then, *post festum*, that the proletariat was 'wavering', not 'mature' enough to act, or even that the development of the productive forces did 'not yet' allow the transition to revolution. That we live in a period of revolution rests – objectively, economically – on the fact that the productive forces have already reached this level of development. If, of course, precisely in the decisive countries, the proletariat is subjectively too immature for revolution, then evidently that has objective, social causes, in whose ranks, however, an extraordinarily large role is played by subjective moments that have become objective moments. (For example, the fact that the first great revolutionary movement of English workers, Chartism, collapsed exactly at the time of the great capitalist boom and before the beginning of the successful economic and trade-union struggles; traditions of the great bourgeois revolution, Proudhonist syndicalism in France; the revolution from 'above' as foundation of national unity and the bourgeois imperialist state – considered economically – in Germany, etc.) If, however, economic development shakes the social foundations of such a state, *then* whether the crisis is fatal or surmountable for the bourgeoisie depends entirely *on the class consciousness of the proletariat.* 'Only when the "lower classes" do not want the old way . . . only then can revolution triumph' (CW 31, p. 85). Does Comrade Rudas believe that this 'will' is just a decorative phrase in Lenin? (In the same fashion that in various places – . . . – he always ironically cites 'the realm of freedom' – he seems to adopt this from Marx and Engels.) That Lenin did not imagine this will in a spontaneous and basal way should be yet another commonplace for a communist. He should know that the vacillation or decisiveness of the masses depends to a large extent on the astute and decisive or cowardly and fatalistic behaviour of the conscious and active vanguard, the Communist Party, the 'form of the proletarian class consciousness' (HCC, p. 333). Here too one utterance from Lenin will suffice: 'That the firm line of the party, its unbending resolution is *just as much a factor* of the mood, particularly in heightened revolutionary situations, is, of course, forgotten "on occasion". Sometimes it is very *convenient* to forget that the obligated leaders through their vacillation and their tendency to forget everything that they offered the day before, import highly indecent swings of mood into certain layers of the masses.'

There are, then, indeed, instants in the process ('moments') where decision is dependent 'only' on the class consciousness of the proletariat. That these moments do not float freely in the air, that they cannot be brought about wilfully, but are occasioned by the objective process, that is to say, they are not to be isolated from the productive process, is evident from the preceding formulations. And according to my understanding, they allow themselves to be so little isolated from the whole process that it is indeed the case that their arrival in the process belongs as an essential characteristic of the process itself. Therefore the Bolshevik and revolutionary (and not tailist) conception of the process itself is determined by the recognition of this connection. Where, namely, the Mensheviks also discern the decisive moments when the active influence of the subjective moment comes to the fore along the lines of a 'gradual development', the decisive moments, as just outlined, must be discovered by the Bolsheviks in the process itself. That means they discover this character of the structure of the process not as an evolutionary one or an organic one, but as contradictory, jerkily unfolding in advances and retreats in every – apparently – calm moment. 'There is no moment,' say the organisational theses of the Third Congress, 'when a Communist Party cannot be active.' Why? Because there can be no moment where this character of the process, the germ, the possibility of an *active* influencing of the subjective moments is completely lacking. 'And what is, for example, each strike other than a small crisis of capitalist society? Wasn't the Prussian Minister of the Interior Mr. von Puttkammer correct when he delivered the famous lines: "In every strike looms the hydra of the revolution!"?' (Lenin, 'Speech on the Revolution of 1905', CW 23, p. 246). Of course, here it is a question of quantity turning into quality. But whoever closes their eyes to the basic question will never be able to grasp properly this side of the process in large-scale events or in small ones. Whoever, like Rudas, out of a tailist fear of falling victim to 'subjectivism', categorically denies such moments will necessarily (as the Hungarian comrades who worked with Comrade Rudas had to find out time after time) react to the more concealed moments in truly fatalistic and tailist ways.

It is clear that such a tailist perspective is irreconcilable with the *preparation* of the revolution, a basic element of Leninism. Comrade Rudas is actually revising Lenin here – of course, quite consciously – in that each time that the matter that he is dealing with pushes towards this concept he foists on it the concept 'anticipation'. 'The proletariat is temporarily too immature to carry out its act of emancipation. Becoming mature depends on many circumstances; among them the role of consciousness of the proletariat plays a certain role, perhaps even a large role. That does not, however, prevent us from anticipating that the proletariat will mature, that the time must come when it fulfils its mission, when it will become aware of it' (*Arbeiterliteratur* X, pp. 696–7). That this is not just a case of a chance stylistic derailment is shown not only by the repetition of this expression, but also by the fact that Comrade Rudas triumphantly parades as a terrible conclusion of my 'subjectivism' the notion that 'the Social Democrats must be correct, then, with their theory that first the proletariat must be educated and cultivated before they can begin to bring about the revolution! The Social Democrats must be correct in their "politics" by restricting all their activity to "educational work"!' (*Arbeiterliteratur* XII, p. 1086). Comrade Rudas obviously thinks that ideological influence is possible only through 'educational work'. Any other influence occurs through the economy, which enters the mind (automatically, without active or conscious activity). Comrade Rudas does not notice just how much of a Kantian he is, how closely he conceives the problem of ideology in a subjective Kantian manner, along the lines of a precise separation of 'pure' from 'practical' reason. I am indeed 'subjectivist' enough not to underestimate educational work, and think it extremely desirable that comrades such as Rudas should thoroughly immerse themselves in Lenin's writings on organisation, before they release an almost Bernsteinian speech against 'subjectivism' in the name of Leninism.

2. Imputation

And so we find ourselves back with one of the foremost sins that I have committed, in Comrade Rudas's opinion. I am talking about so-called 'imputed' class consciousness.

Before I embark on the actual problem, the reader may allow me to make a few introductory remarks. First of all: as with every problem that I have dealt with in my book, I lay no particular weight on the term 'imputation'. If it were to prove to be the case that what I mean by this expression – and still essentially hold to be true today and which I will defend in the words that follow – could be expressed in another way and better, with less room for misunderstandings, I would shed no tears over 'imputation'. If the expression is bad then let it disappear. If I do not follow Rudas, then, in his well-trodden deliberations on the meaning and origin of the word 'imputation' (and intend to speak only about the *matter itself*), I must still note, however, that – whether out of ignorance of the facts or intentionally – he simplifies the matter. He presents the matter as if 'imputation' means a functional dependence, that is to say, as if it were a mathematical term, whose task consists in replacing causality (*Arbeiterliteratur* X, pp. 670ff).[8] This is factually incorrect. 'Imputation' is an old juristic term. If I remember correctly it goes right back to Aristotle. The sense in which I am using the word, however, becomes common only in later jurisprudence. Indeed it comes from an *objectivist* tendency. It is supposed to aid the singling out of the objectively decisive, causal context from the confusion of superficial connections and subjective psychological conditions. For example, an object falls out of a window and kills a passer-by on the street below. From a juristic perspective, who caused the death, and *what* did those concerned do wrong? In the first instance, what is important is not what the person concerned thought or intended, but whether he *could* or *should* have known that his action or failure to act in a normal way *would* have to lead to these consequences. In order not to get myself caught up in what is – for this debate – a peripheral detail, I will refer to a definition, such as is the 'diligens pater familias' of Roman law. It is clear what such definitions are meant to do. They are meant to help reconstruct from the facts the *objectively* essential elements of a legal situation, in order to work out the *objectively* typical elements in such a case. (These objective and typical elements may not coincide in any way at all with what comprises the statistical and average, although it evidently tends in this direction under normal circumstances. However, it is certainly possible, for example, that in an astronomical boom the average speculator does not proceed in accord with the practice of 'normal' merchants, but can still, in spite of that, set a measure for juristic imputation.)

Now – whether consciously or unconsciously – this method is continually being used in the humanities. That is to say, from the facts that are presented to us, the attempt is made to reconstruct the objective situation and 'subjective' moments are explained from this (and not the other way round). By leaving out the inessential details of an objective situation, one can distinguish what people acting according to normal and correct knowledge of their situation were able to do or to allow. According to this measure, their mistakes or their correct insights, etc., can be assessed. I will mention as an example merely Delbrück's war history, for here perhaps Comrade Rudas might be assuaged by Mehring's judgement that learning something from it was not a contamination of his Marxist purity. But, if he reads up on Engels's articles about the war of 1870–71, he can find a similar method in the critique of the campaign by Bourbaki (cf., for example, *Notes on the War*, Vienna 1923). And political critique is no different. The criticism that Marx and Engels levelled at the bourgeois parties in 1848–49 consists –

methodologically – in always showing what they could have done and should have done given the objective economic and political situation and what they, however, failed to do. One might think of the criticism that Marx exercises in the *Eighteenth Brumaire* on the politics of the Montagne and the Party of Order. His analysis of the objective situation does not merely indicate the purely objective impossibility of a certain step or of success (impossibility of proletarian victory in the Junius battle). In certain places, it also shows the subjective incapacity of classes, parties and their leaders to reach possible conclusions from the given situation, and to act accordingly. One example is the analysis of the contest between the unparliamentary ministry of Bonaparte and the Party of Order, when the Minister of the Interior spoke of the threat to the peace. 'It sufficed' – Marx explains – 'for even a mere Vaisse to conjure up the red spectre, and the Party of Order rejected without discussion a motion that would certainly have won for the National Assembly immense popularity and thrown Bonaparte back into its arms. Instead of letting itself be intimidated by the executive power with the prospect of fresh disturbances, it ought rather to have allowed the class struggle a little elbow-room, so as to keep the executive power dependent on itself' (MECW 11, p. 162).

As long as we are only talking about classes, who – because of their objective situation – necessarily act with *false consciousness*, it suffices, in most cases, to counter-balance false consciousness with the objective reality of economic life, in order to grasp correctly the course of the historical process. But even the example that was just cited can teach us that simple counter-balancing is not always sufficient. For 'false consciousness' too can be false in a dialectical and a mechanical way. That is to say, there are objective relations that such a class (given its class position) finds *impossible* to grasp, and, within the same objective relations, there are situations that can be recognised, situations in which it is *possible* to act correctly, consciously or unconsciously (in class terms), in correspondence with the objective situation. The actual thoughts (of classes, parties, leaders) about certain situations, however, do not always match the correct ones that these people should be able to reach from their class position. There is a distance between the consciousness of their situation that they actually possess and the consciousness that they *could* have – given *their* class position. And the prospect of bridging that is the task of parties and their leaders. (I repeat, the second instance of our dilemma does *not* coincide with objectively correct, scientific knowledge of the historical situation; this is only possible on the basis of historical materialism.)

The proletariat finds itself in a different position. The proletariat *can* have a correct knowledge of the historical process and its individual stages, in accordance with its class position. But does it always have this knowledge? Not at all. And inasmuch as this distance is acknowledged to be a *fact*, it is the duty of every Marxist to reflect seriously on its *causes* and – most importantly – on the *means of overcoming* it. This question is the *actual substance* of my difference with Comrade Rudas in relation to the 'imputation' problem. By 'imputed' class consciousness, I mean the consciousness that corresponds to the objective economic position of the proletariat, at any one time, and that can be attained by the proletariat. I used the expression 'imputation' in order to represent this distance clearly. I repeat – while I am quite happy to let the expression go if it leads to misunderstandings – I am not prepared to budge one inch from the *Bolshevik* consideration of class struggle, in order to accommodate mechanistic–tailist objections to the *matter itself*.

As will be well known by the readers of this polemic, my exegesis derives from Marx's phrase (*The Holy Family*): 'It is not a question of what this or that proletarian, or even the whole proletariat, at the moment, *regards* as its aim. It is a question of *what the proletariat is*, and what, in accordance with this *being*, it will historically be compelled to do.' (MECW 4, p. 37.) Comrade Rudas's polemic against my understanding of this paragraph is too easy: that in it is the state of affairs outlined above and, at the same time, that the *task* of the proletarian party is to overcome the distance between being and consciousness, or more precisely: between the consciousness that *objectively corresponds* to the economic being of the proletariat, and a consciousness whose *class character* remains behind this being. According to Rudas's reading, Marx means:

> Socialist authors ascribe a particular world historical role to the proletariat. Why do they do that, and why can they do that? Because today's

society is subjected to certain laws, which prescribe the future direction of society just as necessarily as the direction of a stone that has been thrown is prescribed by the laws of gravity. The stone does not know that its fall is prescribed necessarily by natural forces, and it might just as well be the case that at this moment the proletariat knows nothing of its role either. But only *at the moment* – says Marx. For since the proletariat consists not of stones but of people, who possess consciousness, so they will become aware of their historical mission in time. The English and the French are already beginning to become conscious of their historical tasks. And the others will follow. How do I know that? Because – says Marx – I know as a materialist that consciousness depends on social being, is a product of this social being. Since this being is constituted such that the proletariat through its suffering, etc., is absolutely of necessity forced into action, so too is it absolutely necessary that in time its consciousness will awaken. (*Arbeiterliteratur* X, pp. 695–6)

And the task of 'Marxists', he notes, in accord with the assertion that I have already cited, consists in '*anticipating* this development' (ibid. – Rudas's italics).

Now I believe that Marx would not have been at all satisfied with this 'Marxist' task of 'anticipating', nor with the idea that the proletariat will naturally reach ideological maturity over time. He has voiced his opinions on this matter several times quite unambiguously. I will simply quote here some words from his 'Confidential Reports': 'The English possess all the necessary material preconditions for social revolution. What they lack is a sense of generalisation, and revolutionary passion. Only the General Council is in a position to instil this and to accelerate a truly revolutionary movement in this country and, as a consequence of that, everywhere else' (*Letters to Dr Kugelmann*). Two observations are of great importance for us here. First, that for Marx it appears possible, and therefore clear, that, in his opinion, historical materialism is not contradicted by, but rather confirms that objective ripeness for revolution can be present, while the consciousness of the proletariat *remains behind objective economic development*. Second, that it is the *task* of the International, the international proletarian party to intervene *actively* in the process of developing proletarian class consciousness from its actual position to the highest level that is objectively possible. It is impossible to stress too strongly the fact that, for the matter under consideration here – which is a quite basic *methodological* question of historical materialism – it is of no importance whether Marx was right or wrong in his judgement of the English situation at the time. Opportunists of every stripe always point out Marx's and Engels's 'mistaken' assessment of the situation, their 'overestimation of the revolutionary ripeness' of the situation. Without entering further into this discussion, we must emphasise briefly that the mere fact that a revolution was not achieved is no proof that the objective conditions for a revolution were indeed lacking; witness the Lenin quotation above. We must hold on to the *methodological core* of Marx's assertion. Now, Comrade Rudas – as we have seen – admits as fact the discrepancy in the level of class consciousness of the proletariat. And he does not only prescribe us the 'purely Marxist' formula of 'anticipating' that this fact will naturally and of necessity change over time, but also, at another point in his essay, he backs up this view. 'And if proletarians do not feel more or less "class conscious" or even feel hostile to the class, then that is because their position in the economic process is itself not purely typical. Either they are not working in large factories, or they belong to the petty-bourgeois proletariat' (*Arbeiterliteratur* X, p. 693). Classes are simply fluid forms, says Comrade Rudas, quite correctly; but the result of his formulations is a most incorrect, most undialectical conception of a fluidity flowing of its own accord, without any *conscious assistance* on the part of the Communist Party, naturally and of necessity until a correct understanding of class position 'flows in'. Or, so as not to offend Comrade Rudas's materialist and economistic austerity: these differences will cease if the subjects' position in the economic process becomes 'purely typical'; if, for example, the American workers find employment in large factories, for, as we know, the technical backwardness of the American organisation of the economy is the decisive reason for their undeveloped class consciousness.

But, jokes aside, clearly my aim is not to minimise the significance of this factor. (Cf. on this point HCC, pp. 322–3.) If one considers the whole development of the proletariat from a broad perspective, embracing all epochs, then this perception could even be correct; albeit with some important modifications, which we will go into further shortly.

However, for practical politics – and these are hopefully an important part of Marxist theory for Rudas too – it is not at all correct without qualification. If we start with the beginnings of the independent emergence of the proletariat in Germany, when the workers of precisely the biggest and technically most organised machine factories (Borsig, etc.) held on most tenaciously to organisational unity with the bourgeois and petty-bourgeois parties, while cigar workers, cobblers, tailors, etc., joined the ranks of the revolutionary movement more swiftly (cf., for example, Mehring's *History of the Social Democratic Party*, vol. III), up to the centre workers of the Ruhr district, who were truly not employed in small factories, or the Hungarian movement where Comrade Rudas might have witnessed similar alignments, we can see a similar picture everywhere: the clarity and candour of proletarian self-consciousness is not ranked exclusively, or even at all, according to big concerns and small concerns. And the class consciousness of workers, who work in the same concerns (even if they stem from similar social milieus – if they are not peasants newly moved into the towns or the children of workers), is almost always quite varied. Our consideration of the levels of consciousness in the proletariat must not rest with this obvious and captivating sounding formulation. This alone would necessarily lead to fatalism. (See Comrade Rudas.)

In the passage quoted above, Comrade Rudas alludes to the labour aristocracy, without noticing that he contradicts his own point of view, for the labour aristocracy is recruited – predominantly – out of precisely those layers of the working class who, according to his view, should belong to the 'purest type'. It is recruited from the layer of skilled workers, and mostly those from the largest and technologically most advanced factories. The pre-war theory and practice of the Social Democrats set out from a similar starting point to that of Comrade Rudas. Oblivious to energetic warnings on the part of Marx and Engels, they identified the class consciousness of the labour aristocracy with the class consciousness of the proletariat, and, in cases of conflicts, considered the interests of this layer to be the representative interests of the whole class. Their consciousness was taken to be the appropriate consciousness of the whole class. This follows logically if one conceives class consciousness as a *mechanical* product of the immediate economic position of the workers, if one does not consider social relations in their *totality*. In order to comprehend the function of the labour aristocracy as an obstacle to the development of the revolutionary movement in its entirety, one needs to *abandon immediacy* and recognise the real dialectical forces that bring forth this immediacy and give it its function in the context of the whole. Lenin and his pupils built on and concretised the lessons of Marx and Engels. They recognised the danger that exists for the revolutionary movement if it identifies the interests and the consciousness of this layer of the working class with the class interest and class consciousness of the proletariat. I will cite just one of Lenin's many formulations. Lenin defines opportunism as 'the sacrifice of the basic interests of the mass in favour of the temporary interests of a small number of workers' (*Against the Stream*). In the same spirit, Zinoviev said:

> The narrow corporate interests of this minority of privileged labour aristocrats are what the Social Chauvinists have mistaken for the interests of the working class. This mistake is, incidentally, understandable given the fact that the leaders of the trade unions and the official Social Democratic Party themselves mostly derive from the ranks of the labour aristocracy. The labour aristocracy and the labour bureaucracy are two blood sisters. When the Social Chauvinists speak of the interests of the working class they often – quite unconsciously – have the interests of the labour aristocracy in mind. But even here it is not really a case of true interests in the broader meaning of the term, but rather immediate material advantage. These are absolutely not one and the same thing. (Zinoviev, *The War and the Crisis of Socialism*)

The matter itself is presented with fantastic clarity.

For us, however, desirous of clarity on the *methodological* side of the problem, the following question crops up: with what justification does Comrade Zinoviev maintain that the genuine interests of the working class and immediate material advantage are absolutely not one and the same thing? With what justification does he speak about the 'genuine' interests of the working class at all, refusing to posit this distinction as a 'sociological' one that needs to be traced back to its economic roots, but

rather simultaneously positing one interest (and its corresponding consciousness) as correct, and the other as false and dangerous? (If he found
this passage in my book, Comrade Rudas would start going on indignantly about 'judgement', Rickertian influence, etc.) The answer is
simple: because one consciousness corresponds to the economic and
social position of the class as a totality, while the other sticks at the
immediacy of a particular and temporary interest. But this is just the
starting point of the question. For, first, it is already a matter of a theoretically correct conception of the objective class position, whereby the
crucial point is the *objective correctness* of the theoretical analysis. In and of
itself, both points of view are causal products of social being in human
minds, which are not, *in this respect*, distinguished from each other. Their
difference lies in the extent to which each is a deep or superficial, dialectical or mechanical, practical and critical or fetishistically ideological
analysis of the objective social being, whose product they both are. At
first glance, they appear similar. Their difference only becomes notice-
able when this immediacy is surpassed. Then the objective forms of
mediation that remain hidden in a consciousness trapped in immediacy
are penetrated. This is why a correct theory is not only able to refute a
false one, but is also in a position to point to those moments of existence
that spawn the incorrect theory. It can point out those moments that
representatives of the incorrect theory adopted with unanalysed immediacy and then generalised in a correspondingly abstract way. (That is
why the Bolsheviks are able to explain the social conditions of the advent
of Menshevism, while the Mensheviks in return could only repeat
phrases about putschism, sectarianism, etc.; and this is why Comrade
Lenin, in his polemic about the right to self-determination, uncovered
the historical roots of the mistakes of the Polish and Dutch 'left-
radicals', while simultaneously countering their false theories – *Against the
Stream.*)

Second, a mere analysis of the objective economic situation, even if
theoretically correct, is not enough. The correct *guidelines for action* must
be developed out of the analysis. If, however, the objective economic situation is not immediately apparent in its *objective* correctness, then the
guidelines, and the slogans that follow from them, must be *found* deliberately. In no way do they arise 'spontaneously', and even the spontaneity

of their influence among the workers is in no way a certain criterion of their correctness. (Comrade Lenin points out that under certain circumstances specious 'left' slogans exercise a stronger immediate influence than correct communist slogans, 'but that is', he adds, 'still no proof of the correctness of their tactics' – '*Left-Wing Communism': An Infantile Disorder.*) Precisely the often repeated necessity to swim 'against the stream' – as much in Marx as in Lenin – proves the unfoundedness, the objectively unrevolutionary nature of all 'theories of spontaneity'. But what are then the correct slogans, if they are not simply the thoughts and feelings of the majority of workers, or those of the average worker? They are precisely 'the thoughts and feelings that men would have in a particular situation if they were *able* to assess both it and the interests arising in it in their impact on immediate action and on the whole structure of society. That is to say, it would be possible to infer the thoughts and feelings appropriate to their objective situation' (HCC, p. 51). And so, fortuitously, we have arrived at 'imputed' class consciousness. For that – no more and no less – is what it means to say, irrespective of whether it is called 'imputation' or anything else.

Of course, Comrade Rudas objects: with what justification do I rank precisely this consciousness as class consciousness? 'But' – he says – 'one does not call the consciousness of the proletariat class consciousness because it correctly or falsely reflects their situation. But rather because this consciousness, with all its peculiarities, *is restricted to the proletariat*' (*Arbeiterliteratur* X, p. 690). The second part of the sentence has nothing to do with our argument. Self-evidently both correct and false consciousness are restricted to the proletariat in this case. But any agitator or propagandist could teach Comrade Rudas a lesson on the first part of the sentence. He would ask Comrade Rudas whether he may not speak of class-conscious workers *in contrast* to those who are not class-conscious (who are just as much workers whose thought is just as much determined by their proletarian being). He would ask Comrade Rudas whether he had the right to dispute the proletarian class consciousness of a strike-breaker, indeed even a wavering worker. And, in appealing to the class consciousness of workers through an analysis of the objective situation and the slogans that follow from it, does he have the right to awaken or heighten this class consciousness? Will he be satisfied then with just establishing that economic development has only produced a certain level of class consciousness in the average worker and he – as Marxist – 'anticipates' that this development will gradually develop class consciousness as well to a higher level? With stuff such as this we find ourselves in the swamp of Kautskyist theory, where the 'level of the productive forces' is fate, an attitude that Comrade Stalin has quite rightly labelled a falsification of Marxism. If nothing happens, it is 'because, given the "level of the productive forces" that we had then, nothing else could have been undertaken; the "productive forces" are "to blame" . . . And whoever does not believe this "theory" is simply not a Marxist. The role of the party? Its significance in the movement? But what can the party do in the face of such a crucial factor, as the "level of the productive forces"? . . .' (*Lenin and Leninism*).

Comrade Rudas could perhaps retort: it might occur that, under certain circumstances (although this is not compatible with a spontaneist–tailist perspective), objectively correct theory and the correct slogans that follow from it are not taken up by the workers. It would be, however, the purest idealism to ascribe to this correct knowledge ('a knowledge': *Apage satanas!*) a decisive role in the real class struggle, in actual history. I already responded to this argument when I dealt with the so-called theory of 'moments' and analysed the Marxist–Leninist concept of 'insurrection as an art'. That is why here only a few relevant quotes from Lenin's long list of similar formulations must suffice. Comrade Lenin said at the Eleventh Party Congress of the RCP: 'The communists are a drop in the ocean of people. They will only be in a position to lead the people, to take them down their path, *if they correctly define the path*' (*Speeches at Party Congresses, 1918–1922*, p. 319 – my italics). And, in his '*Left-Wing Communism': An Infantile Disorder*, when he summarises the experiences of the RCP for the benefit of non-Russian communists, he begins his response to the question about the main conditions for the success of the Bolsheviks by emphasising the need for correct theory. All of this belongs to the ABC of Marxism and Leninism, and it is both sad and laughable that I have to explain all of this in such detail. But it has to be done, for now we have hit upon the question of the *party*, a question that for every fan of the spontaneity theory constitutes – consciously or unconsciously – the real stumbling block. (Once more I am referring to the essay by Comrade Rudas on the Hungarian dictatorship.) I concur with Marx: class consciousness is not 'a matter of what this or that proletarian or even the whole proletariat *imagines* for itself as a goal at any point'. Class consciousness is, then, neither a psychological nor a mass-psychological problem, but rather – but here Comrade Rudas interjects indignantly: 'Now one might believe that Comrade Lukács has discovered a third place, where class consciousness realises itself. Perhaps in the head of a God or many gods, perhaps in the head of Madame History, or some such thing' (*Arbeiterliteratur* X, p. 681) – you see, I apparently turn consciousness into a historical demon, a 'demi-urge of actuality, of history' (ibid., p. 687). I am apparently an old Hegelian and so on, and so forth. But let me mollify Comrade Rudas (or, better put, let me upset his tail-ending): this 'third place' is not that difficult *for a communist* to find: it is the *Communist Party*.

We all know the definition that the *Communist Manifesto* gives of communists, and which the Second Congress of the Comintern took up into its theses almost word for word. As a result of that, it has become a commonplace in the Communist Party to appreciate the need for an organisation of class-conscious elements of the proletariat. Sentences that are repeated frequently run the risk of being unquestioningly accepted and echoed, even when, as in this case, they contain nothing but the truth. But what about that moment when they are not repeated word for word, when their true meaning is ignored, indeed when it is declared that they mean exactly their opposite. This is what has happened to Comrade Rudas. Articulating noble indignation, Comrade Rudas gets worked up about the fact that, in the incriminating passage of my book – 'As we stressed in the motto to this essay the existence of this conflict enables us to perceive that class consciousness is identical with neither the psychological consciousness of individual members of the proletariat, nor with the (mass-psychological) consciousness of the proletariat as a whole; but it is, on the contrary, *the sense, become conscious, of the historical role of the class*' (HCC, p. 73) – I confuse consciousness and content of consciousness (*Arbeiterliteratur* X, p. 682). I understand perfectly Comrade Rudas's indignation: his Kantianism that is always arduously repressed has to come up for air now and again and rebel against the practical entwinements of form and content. For it is part of the essence of Kantianism to separate form and content from one another exactly, inflexibly and mechanically, a fact that is very significant in the context of the present discussion:

> whatever happens to be the contents of consciousness, for the thoughts, feelings, aims, etc., which people have may change permanently – in each given period of time they have a complex of these things in their head, and it is this complex that is called 'consciousness'. And this consciousness can *only* be realised in the individual person psychologically or, in the many, mass-psychologically. What this 'psychological or mass-psychological realisation' means is decided by another science, and to be precise a natural science, psychology (mass psychology). (Ibid., pp. 682–3)

To put it simply: the content of consciousness is a 'sociological question', consciousness itself is a 'psychological' question; both questions have only a loose, distant and complicated relationship to one another, for they belong to 'different sciences'. Comrade Rudas says:

> Only that which becomes conscious for them, that is to say, only the content of consciousness is further defined by Lukács in the second part of the passage: that is the 'sense of the historical role of the class'. But that is a different situation, if you please! What the content of consciousness of the person is at any one moment, whether this content corresponds to reality or not, that is a question in itself, which has absolutely nothing at all to do with the question of whether consciousness is psychological or mass-psychological! May the content be true or false, expressing a 'sense of the historical role of the class' or not, the consciousness that accommodates this content is either an individual psychological or mass-psychological one! (Ibid., p. 682)

Anyway, Comrade Rudas thinks that an explanation of the relationship of 'psychology' to Marxism might be an 'extremely interesting' question, but in the way that he phrases this question it is extremely unlikely that anything sensible would come of it.

If we attempt to move away from the schematic, Kantian treatment of the question in Rudas, then we have to ask if class consciousness (for class consciousness and not consciousness in general is what is under investigation here!) is an issue that really can be treated *separately* from the *content* of consciousness? The formulations expressed so far have already shown that this is impossible. Let us go back to the previous example. If we deny that a strike-breaker has proletarian class consciousness then we are neither denying that he is a worker according to his social being, nor that within him (in his worker's head, Comrade Rudas!) a process of consciousness is taking place (even a causally necessary process of consciousness) that has led to the strike-breaking. We are simply contesting whether the content of *his consciousness corresponds to his objective class position*. For a dialectician, the concept of consciousness is necessarily *inseparable* from its content. It is a *concrete* concept, while the Kantian – however carefully he disguises himself as a materialist – will always seek a general, formal definition (in Comrade Rudas's case this is the psychological), which can be related to an arbitrary content whose explanation is a task for 'another science'. And because he is absolutely unable to imagine a dialectical relationship between content and form, a determination of form by content, a correspondingly dialectically changing form, his noble indignation is (psychologically or – if Comrade Rudas prefers it – mass-psychologically) quite understandable. For it follows necessarily from his mechanical dualistic perspective that this 'third place' where class consciousness is realised can only be a 'demon' or a 'god', since this 'third place' has to remain transcendent for mechanistic and dualistic thought. The real social basis is, of course, tail-ending, in whose eyes the party is always somewhat transcendent.

If, however, one refuses to follow the Kantian separation of form and content slavishly, in the manner of Comrade Rudas, then the question is really quite simple. We repeat: the concept of class consciousness is one that contains content. It is a concrete concept and the famous 'third place' where the concept is realised is *the organisation of the Communist Party*. Comrade Lenin clearly emphasised this task of the party from the very beginning and defended it clearly versus tailist disciples of the theory of spontaneity. He puts it thus: 'If it is to be a conscious spokesman *in fact*, the party must be able to work out such organisational relations as will *ensure a definite level* of consciousness and systematically raise this level' (*One Step Forward, Two Steps Back*, CW 7, p. 273). Of course, this process takes place inside party members' heads. But this alone, however, cannot settle the question decisively, for opportunistic perspectives and forms of organisation take place as much inside the heads of opportunists as revolutionary ones take place inside the heads of revolutionaries, *formally* in the psychological sense. Both perspectives are just as 'conscious' or just as little 'conscious'. Thus Rosa Luxemburg, as representative of the theory of spontaneity, consistently, that is to say consistently incorrectly, could say: 'Since however the Social Democratic movement is a mass movement and the threatening obstacles stem not from people's heads but from social conditions, opportunistic aberrations cannot be prevented . . . Regarded from this perspective opportunism appears to be a product of the workers' movement itself, and an inevitable phase of its historical development' ('Organisational Questions of Russian Social Democracy' in *Rosa Luxemburg Speaks*, ed. Mary Alice Waters (New York, 1970), p. 129). But, really, the decisive question is *how*, on the one hand, correct recognition of the class position of the proletariat ('level of consciousness' in Lenin, 'sense of the historical role of the class' in me) can be raised to an ever higher level, that is to say, become ever more correct in terms of content, ever more appropriate to the actual situation. And, on the other hand, how this consciousness can be *made* conscious in as large a section of the class as possible (ensuring and raising of the level in Lenin).

Of course this relationship must be conceived as a relationship between permanently moving moments, as a process. (I hope that the dialectical meaning of the word 'process' has already been adequately explained so that there is no more room for the tailist suppression of evidence.) This means that economic being, and, with it, proletarian class consciousness and its organisational forms, find themselves transformed uninterruptedly. In the process, the determinations sketched here are valid for every moment of this process of transformation, and are, in each phase, products of the previous phase and, at the same time, determinate causes of the coming phase. That is why determinations such as level of class consciousness, the sense of historical role are not abstract and formal, not concepts that are fixed for all time, but express concrete relationships in concrete historical situations. 'The fact that proletarian class consciousness becomes autonomous and assumes objective form is only meaningful for the proletariat if at every moment it really embodies for the proletariat the revolutionary meaning of precisely that moment' (HCC, p. 333). This development, this raising of the level of class consciousness is, then, not an endless (or finite) progress, not a permanent advance towards a goal fixed for all time, but itself a dialectical process. Not only does it take place in uninterrupted interchange with the development of social reality in its totality (for example, an unsuccessful action of the proletariat, caused by vacillation or the low level of consciousness of the vanguard, can change the objective situation in such a way that further development – in a certain sense – sets in at a lower level), but correspondingly it does not proceed in an unequivocal, upwards rising line. Precisely, Bolshevik self-criticism with its unprecedented significance for the development of parties, and mediated to the whole proletariat through those parties, shows this most clearly. For what does self-criticism mean – methodologically? The knowledge that the actions of the party, at any given moment, were not on the same level as might have been objectively possible in the given situation. In examining the causes of this discrepancy in level between actual activity and its concrete and objective possibility, one must not stick simply to establishing the objective cause, for such 'objectivism', as Comrade Zinoviev correctly points out (*Against the Stream*) looks, at best, like fatalism. Examination of the causes of a mistake is, on the contrary, directed towards the eradication of the causes. Which is why it is utterly possible that the development of the level of class consciousness can be more strongly encouraged through mistakes that are correctly recognised and, correspondingly, thoroughly corrected, than through a partially correct activity that has, however, merely arisen spontaneously.

Lenin's *organisational forms* are essential for this. In no way are they, as Comrade Rosa Luxemburg thought, useless 'paper' guarantees. On the contrary, they are a decisive moment in the emergence and further development of proletarian class consciousness. The organisational forms of the proletariat, in first rank the party, are real *forms of mediation*, in which and through which develops and *is* developed the consciousness that corresponds to the social being of the proletariat. The organisational forms of the proletariat arise, in part, spontaneously, from the base, out of the class struggle, and in part they are created, in (correct or false) consciousness. If, however, the spontaneous basal mode of emergence is understood to be the only possible one, or the only correct one, then the danger arises that the mediating function of organisational form will be left out of the picture. On the one hand, organisation is underestimated, and deliverance is brought about only by the spontaneous mass movement, who also create organisational forms (Rosa Luxemburg, op. cit.) while the organisation is demoted to an inhibiting, 'conservative moment' (ibid.). On the other hand, an organisation conceived in this way and led in this way does indeed develop conservative and inflexible moments, which disconnect it from living, permanently changing historical existence. Both sides of the question are closely connected. If bourgeois sociologists, for example Michels, bring out this 'conservative' moment of 'party sociology', then, from a bourgeois point of view, they are operating quite consistently and overlook, of course, just as consistently the *specificity* of proletarian class organisation. And Comrade Rudas who, on the question of proletarian class consciousness, *that is to say*, on the question of organisation, privileges a Kantian dualism of form and content that hopes to solve the question of class consciousness in a 'general' psychological or sociological way, acts just as consistently, when at every turn he adopts a purely contemplative, reflective perspective in respect of history, when he – of course without admitting it, indeed perhaps without even being aware of it – stands continuously in the camp of spontaneity theory. For, seen from a methodological point of view, spontaneity theory is nothing other than a way of seeing that, applied to the class struggle of the proletariat, sets out (supposedly) from the class standpoint of the proletariat, and yet is contemplative, that is, bourgeois, dualistic and undialectical.

What is the significance of my labelling the organisation a real form of mediation? Once again it is part of the ABC of Marxism, but, unfortunately, has to be repeated yet again: the actual make-up of social phenomena is *not immediately* apparent. The direct forms of appearance of social being are not, however, subjective fantasies of the brain, but moments of the real forms of existence, the conditions of existence of capitalist society. It seems obvious to the people who live in capitalist society, indeed it strikes them as 'natural', to stick with these forms and not to strive to fathom the more hidden interconnections (intermediary terms, mediations) through which these phenomena interconnect in reality, and through whose identification they can be understood only in their *correct context*. If Comrade Rudas (*Arbeiterliteratur* X, pp. 673–4) conceives Marxism simply as an empirical science,[9] then he falls victim to – to put it mildly – bourgeois one-sidedness, since he sets empirical and aprioristic ways of seeing inflexibly and dualistically against each other in a Kantian manner. It is true that Marx stresses the empirical character of historical materialism in contrast to the constructive philosophy of history. Nevertheless, countering economic empiricism, he emphasises, for example, that 'all science would be superfluous if outward appearance and the essence of things directly coincided' (*Capital* III, Ch. 48, MECW 37, p. 804) and he stresses that Ricardo's main error is 'not going far enough, [. . .] not carrying his abstraction to completion' (*Theories of Surplus Value* II (London, 1969), p. 106). And these correct abstractions, as is known, do not grow directly in empirical reality like blackberries, commonplaces and Comrade Rudas's fraternally embraced donkeys (*Arbeiterliteratur* XII, p. 1070).[10] (In his enthusiasm about fraternising with the donkey, Comrade Rudas overlooks the catholicising, Franciscan, Biedermeier-style facets of F. Jammes's 'materialist soul'.) They are also in no way so independent from the *standpoint* of theory as Comrade Rudas (*Arbeiterliteratur* X, p. 673) assumes.[11] Of course their discernibility does not depend on any 'aim of knowledge' in a bourgeois sense, but rather on the class standpoint and the 'aims of knowledge' that are conditioned by it. In the criticisms that Marx voices against Smith or Ricardo one can read what role their class standpoint and the knowledge aims determined by it play in their – often empirically correct – conception of actuality. (I am deliberately not speaking about the apologists here.) If, in contrast to this, historical materialism alone is in a position to offer objective and correct knowledge of capitalist society, it does not deliver this knowledge independently of the class standpoint of the proletariat, but rather *precisely from this standpoint*. Whoever is unable to see this interconnection, and therefore separates historical materialism from the class standpoint of the proletariat, is either an undialectical dualist (who separates theory from praxis *à la*

Hilferding) or an idealist (like Lassalle). Comrade Rudas seems to belong to both groups alternately. The consequences that flow from an idealist, undialectical linking of class standpoint and historical materialism will be dealt with later.

Lenin worked out the concrete possibilities of *proletarian praxis*, through detection of the *real links of mediation* between class position and conscious correct praxis – this must count as one of his undying theoretical achievements. (Whereas Rosa Luxemburg, to cite a contrasting example, clung to an unmediated and mythological way of seeing.) For the class consciousness of the proletariat is never supplied directly, neither in terms of its content nor in its emergence and development. For as long as the real mediating links of its growth remain unrecognised, and therefore unanalysed in practical terms, it develops spontaneously and elementally. (The effectiveness of unrecognised real social forces assumes, as form of consciousness, a spontaneous character.) And in order to abolish this spontaneity it is not at all sufficient to recognise the general, economic and social forms of existence which bring out and determine class consciousness, not even if they are worked out economically right down to the smallest detail. Rather, those *specific* real forms of mediation that are suited to promote *this* process or to inhibit it – of course, on the basis of and in connection with the whole process of economic development – must be recognised concretely and applied concretely. Marx is not only the author of *Capital* but also the founder of the Communist League and the First International. And Lenin is especially in this respect his greatest, indeed his only pupil of equal standing; he is the founder of the Russian Communist Party, the Third International; and, verily, not just as a 'theoretical development' but precisely as an *organisational form*.

From the very beginning the organisational forms recognised and applied by Lenin were resisted by – and are still today resisted by – all opportunists as 'artificial' forms. The reason is easy to see – it is the *same* reason that the tail-ender Rudas wheels out of his mind in order to counter my definition of class consciousness. These organisational forms, namely, are not simply mental formulations of the unmediated state of consciousness of the average worker (even if his situation is 'thoroughly typical'). That is to say, they are 'neither psychological nor

mass-psychological' perceptions, but work out rather practical measures from a correct knowledge of the historical process as a whole, from
the totality of its economic, political, ideological, etc., moments. These
practical measures are those with whose help, on the one hand *one part* of
the proletariat is raised to the level of consciousness that correctly corresponds to its objective position in the totality, while, on the other hand,
the broad mass of workers and other exploited people can be led correctly in their struggles. It must be underlined at once that only a part of
the workers can be raised to this level. Lenin says it repeatedly: '. . . it
would be Manilovism and "tail-ending" to think that at any time under
capitalism the entire class, or almost the entire class, would be able to
rise to the level of consciousness and activity of its vanguard, of its
Social Democratic party' (from: *One Step Forward, Two Steps Back*.
'Paragraph One of the Rules').[12] But even in this portion of the working
class consciousness does not only not arise 'by itself', but not even as an
immanent result of its immediate economic position and the inevitable
class struggles that develop from it at the base. As Lenin explains – in
What is to be Done?: 'Correct class consciousness' (he uses the term social-
democratic consciousness here) 'would have to be brought to them from
without. The history of all countries shows that the working class, exclusively by its own effort, is able to develop only trade-union consciousness,
that mean conviction of the necessity of organising as trade unionists,
i.e., the conviction that it is necessary to combine in unions, fight the
employers, and strive to compel the government to pass necessary labour
legislation, etc.' (*What is to be Done?*, CW 5, p. 375). However, this is a
historical process, and the spontaneous element is the germ seed of a
conduct that is conscious of its aims (ibid.). Moreover the transition
cannot take place elementally.

In spite of this, there is, of course, a dialectical interrelationship
between this 'from without' and the working class. For while Marx and
Engels stem from the bourgeois class, the development of their doctrine
is, nevertheless, a product of the development of the working class – of
course not in any immediate way. And not only the doctrine itself; even
elements of its foundation (Ricardo, Hegel, French historians and
socialists) more or less consciously summarise in thought that social
being out of which and as a part of which the proletariat arose. With

the predecessors of Marx and Engels, it is only this objective social foundation of existence that combines theory and class struggle, such that – in immediate terms – they appear to run side by side independently, until theory becomes 'a conscious product of historical movement' and with that becomes revolutionary (*Poverty of Philosophy*). But – according to Lenin's profound and correct conception – even this theory influences the proletariat from without. And even if the economic development of society makes possible a proletarian party founded on this theory, its influence on the spontaneous movements of the class will still come – albeit, of course, quite decisively dialectically qualified – 'from outside'. For it would be un-Marxist to think that as long as capitalism exists (and even for some time afterwards) the whole working class can 'spontaneously' reach the level of consciousness that corresponds objectively to its objective economic position. Development consists in the fact that this 'from outside' the class is brought ever closer to the class, such that it loses its exterior character, without being able – given the present stage of development – to abolish the dialectical relationship that Lenin pinpoints. For the social being of the proletariat places it *immediately* only in a relationship of struggle with the capitalists, while proletarian class consciousness becomes class consciousness proper when it incorporates a knowledge of the *totality* of bourgeois society. At another point in the same piece of writing Lenin explains this thought in the following way: 'Class political consciousness can be brought to the workers *only from without*, that is, only from outside the economic struggle, from outside the sphere of relations between workers and employers. The sphere from which alone it is possible to obtain this knowledge is the sphere of relationships of *all* classes and strata to the state and the government, the sphere of the interrelations between all classes.' And he adds: 'the spontaneous struggle of the proletariat will not become its genuine "class struggle" until the struggle is led by a strong organisation of revolutionaries' (CW 5, p. 423). And this organisation is comprised of people who have *recognised* this, and who want to work actively in this direction, professional revolutionaries: 'in view of this common characteristic of all members of such an organisation, all distinctions as between workers and intellectuals, not to speak of distinctions of trade and profession, in both categories, must be effaced' (ibid.) Therefore, for Lenin the revolutionary social democrat is 'a Jacobin who maintains an inseparable bond with the *organisation* of the proletariat, a proletariat conscious of its class interests' (*One Step Forward, Two Steps Back*, CW 7, p. 381).

Well then? So this mysterious 'third place', this 'historical demon', the Communist Party – which even to invoke just as a possibility seems impossible to the tail-ender Rudas – possesses a curious characteristic: it is a *content* that is necessarily tied to becoming conscious. That means that, on the one hand, it depends on the content become conscious whether the consciousness that thinks can be recognised as conscious (class conscious), while, on the other hand, *at the same time*, the content must become conscious, must become effective in the heads of people, in order to be realised. Forms of organisation are there in order to bring this process into being, to accelerate it, in order *to make* such contents conscious in the working class (in a part of the working class), which once made conscious turn the workers into class-conscious workers, precisely those contents that correspond as adequately as possible to their objective class situation. Here we can see that 'simple contradiction' which Comrade Rudas (*Arbeiterliteratur* X, p. 679) finds in this definition of class consciousness, as a *dialectical state of affairs*;[13] that is to say it is only saddled with a contradiction – a dialectical contradiction – to the extent that the reality that underlies it is itself dialectical and contradictory. And the 'idealism' that he accuses me of (ibid.) proves to be the *Bolshevik form of organisation of the class-conscious proletariat*. The discrepancy between the 'process' and its 'sense' (ibid.) is not at all, as Comrade Rudas would have me say, a discrepancy between causal connection and 'purpose', but rather the difference between the immediately given, empirical reality of the working class (in whom, Comrade Lenin explains, has grown up only a trade-union consciousness) and the concretely developing totality of all social determinations, which occasion this immediate reality. Comrade Rudas might easily have grasped what is meant by this difference if he had been in a position to read the relevant passages in my book without tailist prejudice: out of the analysis of the relationship between momentary particular interests and class interests which follows on directly from that and which culminates in the Marxist distinction between trade-union struggles and the real emancipation of the proletariat. For any unbiased reader, the term 'sense' means here nothing other than, on the one hand, highlighting this distinction, and the other hand, and *at the same time*, that this difference points to the forms of mediation of activity, of praxis, that is to say, of real class consciousness. The 'contradiction' that is supposed to exist here is present only for the non-dialectical thinker. For him a contradiction issues from the 'objectivity' of this class consciousness (i.e. its content, its real forms of mediation *are not determined* by its being thought) and its 'subjectivity' (i.e. the contents become conscious, the form of consciousness must be taken up in order to become real). Of course, if form and content are mechanically separated from each other, in Kantian fashion, then their dialectical interrelationship must appear incomprehensible.

Since content separated from consciousness in this way is only a kind of channel through which objective processes flow in full spontaneity, Comrade Rudas evidently finds it incomprehensible that I hold the emergence of proletarian class consciousness to be a decisive, indeed under certain conditions, the most decisive question of historical development. 'But up until now nobody has yet called the class struggle of the proletariat a struggle for consciousness' (*Arbeiterliteratur* XII, p. 1081). I do not want to pile up quotes pointlessly and so I will simply cite something said by Comrade Zinoviev: 'The communist vanguard of the working class struggles against social democracy (labour aristocracy, petit bourgeois fellow travellers) *for the working class*. The working class, at whose head stands the Communist Party, struggles with the bourgeoisie *for the peasantry*' ('Proletariat and Peasantry', *Inprekorr* V, no. 5). Does Comrade Rudas think that this is not a struggle over consciousness? If at all possible, Comrade Lenin and his pupils refuse violent measures against the peasantry. They hope to *convince* the peasantry of the necessity of forming an alliance with the proletariat – and it would be useful to find out whether here too consciousness is only a channel and from where and to where the 'process' spontaneously flows. Comrade Rudas's mistakes become understandable if we remind ourselves that, by influence on consciousness, he only understands 'educational work' (and that in its social-democratic sense). A conception that he will not find in Marx, in Lenin, nor in me. Every Bolshevik knows exactly that 'the struggle over consciousness' embraces the whole activity of the party, that its struggle against the class enemy is *inseparable* from the struggle *for* the class consciousness of the proletariat and *for* making conscious the alliance with the semi-proletarian layers (as much in these layers as in the proletariat). For the consciousness of the masses at any one time does not develop independently of the party's politics, and the class consciousness embodied in it.

> It is self-evident that the actions of the class are largely determined by its average members. But as the average is not static and cannot be determined statistically, but is itself the product of the revolutionary process, it is no less self-evident that an organisation that bases itself on an existing average is doomed to hinder development and even to reduce the general level. Conversely, the clear establishing of the highest possibility *objectively* available at a given point in time, as represented by the autonomous organisation of the conscious vanguard, is itself a means by which to relieve the tension between this objective possibility and the actual state of consciousness of the average members in a manner advantageous to the revolution. (HCC, p. 327)

And Lenin derives the potential wavering of the mood of the masses (their psychological or mass-psychological consciousness) precisely at a decisive moment from the behaviour of the party; compare the example cited earlier from 'Letter to a Comrade'.

3. *The peasantry as class*

Of course, everything that has been said here relates to the consciousness of the proletariat. And this is another point that excites the noble indignation of Comrade Rudas. His 'exact' and 'scientific' soul demands that consciousness (the form of consciousness precisely separated from its contents) must be examined in a psychological laboratory, while the questions of content are obviously to be left to – a just as 'exact' – 'sociology'. However, for this sociology – self-evidently! – the class consciousness of all classes, of all times is simply class consciousness; a form of consciousness that is called forth by the economic situation. At night all cows are black. He notes 'only in passing' (*Arbeiterliteratur* X, p. 691) my doubt as to whether peasants can be labelled a class at all in the strict Marxist sense of the term. This observation refers to one passage in my book (HCC, p. 61), whereby Comrade Rudas 'forgets' to quote the previous page, for there, indeed I cite from the *Eighteenth Brumaire*:

> In so far as millions of families live under economic conditions of existence that separate their mode of life, their interests and their culture from those of the other classes, and put them in hostile opposition to the latter, they form a class. In so far as there is merely a local interconnection among these small-holding peasants, and the identity of their interests begets no community, no national bond and no political organisation among them, they do not form a class. (MECW 11, p. 187)

This view is still today the communist view. In his theses on the peasant question (accepted at the last session of the expanded ECCI, *Inprekorr* V, no. 77) Comrade Bukharin formulated the class position of the peasants exactly along the lines of the passage just quoted:

> The peasantry, which in the past was the basic class of feudal domination, is not a class in the actual sense of the word in capitalist society . . . Therefore taken as a *whole* the peasantry is not a class in capitalist society. But in so far as we are dealing with a society that is in transition from relations of a feudal character to production relations of a capitalist character, the peasantry as a *whole* frequently finds itself in a contradictory position: in relation to the feudal landed possessors it is a class, but inasmuch as it is in the grip of and displaced by capitalist relationships, it ceases to be a class.

This matches exactly the economic analysis of Marx who saw the bourgeoisie and the proletariat as the typical, real classes of bourgeois society, whose expansion tends to reduce the whole society to these two classes. In line with this conception, Marx analyses the social being of the peasantry: 'As owner of the means of production he is capitalist; as labourer he is his own wage-labourer' (*Theories of Surplus Value* I, p. 408). And by going through all the contradictions that follow from this, he indicates the fundamental contradiction in the social being of the peasantry. In any case: in capitalist society every social being must rest on a contradiction. One would be un-Marxist, abstract, acting in accordance with the methods of merely formal bourgeois 'sociology' if one remained at the level of the simple, abstract concept of contradiction. Contradiction is not always simply contradiction, and all cows are black actually only in the night of bourgeois thought. The contradiction in the economic basis of existence of both the typical classes of capitalist society (whereby we are now – for the sake of contrast – not forgetting for a minute the difference between the bourgeoisie and the proletariat dealt with so thoroughly in my book) means that this economic base progresses in contradictions. It means that its development is always an ever broader and deeper unfolding, an ever more expanded reproduction of the *immanent* contradictions of the foundations (crisis). That does not, however, mean that this economic basis that progresses through contradictions is split into *heterogeneous parts*. It means that the *dialectical* contradictions of the capitalist order of production come to light in the social being (and consequentially in the consciousness too) of the bourgeoisie and the proletariat, but not in the *contradictions between two different orders of production*, as with the peasants. The contradictions of such a social being as that of the peasantry are, therefore, not immediately dialectical, like the contradictions of capitalist society itself, but they become dialectical only in a *mediated* way through the dialectic of the total development of capitalist society. Therefore it is only from a class standpoint that they can be grasped as dialectical, can be made conscious, a standpoint that – as a result of the social being that lays at its basis – is in a position to understand the total development of capitalist society as a dialectical process. That is to say, from the standpoint of the proletariat. The standpoint of bourgeois class is unable to recognise this total movement (that is the necessary development of capitalism from pre-capitalist forms of production, the necessity of the development of this form of production alongside capitalism, the necessity of the transition of this total complex into socialism, etc.). If, at points, the bourgeoisie has also acted – economically and politically – correctly in class terms, then it has done this, however, with 'false consciousness'. 'We are not aware of this, nevertheless we do it,' Marx once said of bourgeois praxis (*Capital* I, MECW 35, p. 85).

And what of the peasants themselves? Let us look at their social being rather more closely from the standpoint of Marxist theory. Directly before the passage that I quoted earlier, Marx says: 'They (the peasants) therefore belong neither to the category of *productive* nor of *unproductive labourers*, although they are producers of commodities. But their production does not fall under the capitalist mode of production' (*Theories of Surplus Value* I, p. 407). He explains this state of affairs more concretely in another passage: 'In the first place, the general laws of credit are not adapted to the farmer, since these laws presuppose a capitalist as the producer' (*Capital* III, ch. 47, MECW 37, p.1085). In what follows he goes on to provide a thorough overview of this situation. I will cite only the most important sentences:

> On the other hand, this development takes place only where the capitalist mode of production has a limited development and does not unfold all of its peculiarities, because this rests precisely upon the fact that agriculture is no longer, or not yet, subject to the capitalist's mode of production, but rather to one handed down from extinct forms of society. The disadvantages of the capitalist mode of production, with its dependence of the producer upon the money-price of his product, coincide here therefore with the disadvantages occasioned by the imperfect development of the capitalist mode of production. The peasant turns merchant and industrialist without the conditions enabling him to produce his products as commodities. (ibid., pp. 1086–7)

And in conclusion he says of the smallholding that it 'creates a class of barbarians standing halfway outside of society' (ibid.). What is the consequence of all this? Not at all Comrade Rudas's assertion that I say the peasants do not constitute a class at all. Certainly though there is an essentially different concrete relation between their social being and their consciousness compared to other classes; presupposing that we do not – as does a good Kantian like Comrade Rudas – stick to the pure formula that, in any case, social being (in general) determines consciousness (in general), but rather seek to understand how this being determines the *concrete particularity* of this *specific* social being. I have attempted to characterise this particularity by finding – in contrast to the dialectical contradiction between class consciousness and class interest with the bourgeoisie – a contradictory contradiction (HCC, p. 61). I do not, I hope, need to repeat what I have already [said] about class consciousness (but just to be on the safe side I point once more to the 'in so far' of Marx on the peasantry as a class, to the theses of Bukharin and the view of Lenin on *when* the immediate economic struggle of the proletariat too can be termed class struggle). The immediate day-to-day interests of the working class arise from their social being in such a way that they *can* be linked to the wider interests of the class as a whole with correct consciousness, although as we have seen, according to Lenin's view, this does not come about of its own accord. In the case of the bourgeoisie, a corresponding linking is possible only on the basis of 'false consciousness' (whereby once again I must point out the expressly dialectical character of this 'false consciousness'). For the peasantry such a linking is – from its own class point of view – not at all possible. Rudas introduces various statements from Lenin to counter my conception (as he understands it) (*Arbeiterliteratur* X, p. 691).[14] Whoever studies these sentences closely will find that without exception they speak in my favour and against Rudas. Comrade Lenin points, for example – just as Marx does in the passages above – to the fact that the peasant 'is half-worker and half-speculator'. What is then the consequence of that for the peasantry's praxis? Even Comrade Rudas admits: 'It is just as clear that the peasants cleave at one point to the capitalists, and at another point to the workers' (ibid., p. 692). But: does this wavering really *correspond* to their correctly understood *class interests* or does it rather mirror the fact that the peasants – in relation to their immediate momentary interests – are 'realists', hardboiled empiricists, but in terms of their class situation, *only* empiricists, who are unable to hold properly in view the real issues of their own class as a whole? Does it prove that at best their class consciousness has reached only that *level* that Comrade Lenin, in relation to the proletariat, called trade-union consciousness – *in contrast* to proletarian class consciousness? What I claimed was precisely this: the peasants cannot have a class consciousness that corresponds to the level of the proletarian one. In light of their class position, they are *objectively incapable* of leading and organising the *whole* society on the basis of and in line with their class interests. The contradiction of their social being (*half*-worker and *half*-speculator) is mirrored in their consciousness: 'Inasmuch as only a local contiguity exists amongst peasants with plots of land, the unity of their interests creates amongst them no community, no national ties, and no political organisation. They do not form a class.' One is reminded of Engels's presentation of the strategy of the peasant war – just to allay another objection of Rudas while we are at it. I said: 'But it often turns out that questions of class consciousness prove to be decisive in just those situations where force is unavoidable and classes are locked in a life-and-death-struggle' (HCC, p. 53). Comrade Rudas thinks (*Arbeiterliteratur* XII, pp. 1070–1) that this conception contradicts that of the military theorist Engels.[15] He should read *Peasant War* carefully for once. Engels remarks of military decision (and *only* this was up for discussion):

> Truchsess's cunning saved him here from certain ruin. Had he not succeeded in fooling the weak, limited, for the most part demoralised peasants and their usually incapable, timid and venal leaders, he would have been closed in with his small army between four columns numbering at least from 25,000 to 30,000 men, and would have perished. It was the narrow-mindedness of his enemies, always inevitable among the peasant masses, that made it possible for him to dispose of them at the very moment when, with one blow, they could have ended the entire war, at least as far as Swabia and Franconia were concerned. (*The Peasant War in Germany*, ch. 5, MECW 10, p. 459)

One is reminded also of Stambulisky's leadership, to use an example from the recent past.[16] This is interesting for two reasons, for, on the one hand, the incapacity of the peasants to lead is drastically apparent, and, on the other hand, precisely the mistakes of the Communist Party make clear how the peasants can and must be shown their *own* way by the proletariat alone.

One would not say that the proletariat has not acted wrongly in many situations. I admit it. But the proletariat is able to develop further, to reach a real class consciousness that is no longer merely a trade-union consciousness, objectively, *through its own power*. The peasantry has to be *led*. It should be self-evident that this leadership is not carried out forcibly, and that thereby a continual interaction takes place between the transformation of social being and the consciousness of the peasantry. However: the dialectical contradictions of the development as a whole become conscious *in* the proletariat (or the party). The proletariat *mediates* for the peasants the link to further evolution, an evolution that corresponds to the social being and corresponding development of consciousness of the peasants, but would not be locatable by this consciousness. This passage relates to such classes: 'it might turn out that the masses were in the grip of quite different forces, that they were in pursuit of quite different ends. In that event there might be a purely coincidental connection between the theory and their activity, it would be a form that enables the masses to become conscious of their socially necessary or coincidental actions, without ensuring a genuine and necessary bond between consciousness and action' (HCC, p. 2),[17] wherefrom Comrade Rudas derives my idealism, along with other things (*Arbeiterliteratur* IX, pp. 505–6).[18] He forgets thereby that for the dialectical method – indeed for it alone – 'coincidentally' in no way means something causally unnecessary. On the contrary: coincidence is the form of appearance of a given type of causal determination. If Rudas is not familiar with Hegel, he might know it from Engels. Coincidence is, according to Engels, 'only one pole of an interrelation, the other pole of which is called necessity' (MECW 26, p. 273; cf. also Marx's Letter to Dr Kugelmann, 17.4.1871). That the consciousness appropriate to the social being of the peasants is established by the proletariat and is mediated to the peasantry by the proletariat and is activated in them by the proletariat, and that the peasantry must be led by the proletariat, that on their own they can only act 'spontaneously', 'coincidentally', does not mean by a long chalk that the peasantry has no consciousness that springs of necessity from its social being. It is just that this is not class consciousness in the sense in which *only* the proletariat *can* possess it. Therefore the points when the proletariat connects with the development of the peasantry need not necessarily be always the economically most expedient moments of development. On the contrary. The doctrinal mistakes of the young Communist Parties (e.g. the Hungarian party in the dictatorship) consisted precisely in the fact that their starting point was the objective economic superiority of the modern managed agricultural large-scale industry, and they overlooked the fact that it is only after prolonged revolutionary instruction that the peasantry can be brought to understand the advantage (for the peasantry!) that this large-scale organisation means economically. We overlooked – doctrinally – the specific forms of development, the specific forms of mediation of consciousness of the peasants. Comrade Lenin keenly and repeatedly drew our attention to this point: 'Right up until today they have stuck to this prejudice against large-scale agriculture. The peasant thinks: "large-scale agriculture – I will be a land worker again". *Of course this is wrong*. But for the peasants the idea of large-scale agriculture is bound up with hatred, with the memory of how the population were oppressed by the landowners. This feeling persists. It is not dead' ('On Work in the Countryside; Speech at the 8th Congress of the RCP', CW 29, p. 210 – my italics). But to comply with this *utterly correct* politics in the case of the proletariat would mean the same as making concessions to the extant syndicalist tendencies of broad layers of the workers, and would encourage just such a sinking of the level that Lenin justifiably saw as an essential characteristic of opportunism. Methodologically, to recognise this difference means: to recognise that the relationship between social being and class consciousness in the proletariat and in the peasantry is *structurally* different. And our theory treats the different forms of consciousness of different classes concretely and dialectically, in historically dialectical ways, and not in formal sociological ways or formal psychological ways.

I hope that with all this I have sufficiently explained my use of the term 'imputation'. I will not go into the ins and outs, the sauce that Comrade Rudas serves with his tailist cabbage. He knows very well that I have broken with my past completely, not only socially but also philosophically, that I consider the writings that I wrote before my entry into the Hungarian Communist Party to be mistaken and wrong in every way. (Of course that in no way means that I hold everything that I have written since 1918 to be correct today. The selection that I made in 1922 in the edition of HCC is also a criticism of earlier writings.) Comrade Rudas also knows perfectly well that, for example, I have never accepted that there is a general human consciousness. He knows my position on Max Adler (cf. my critique in *Wjestnik der Sozialistischen Akademie* 1923, pamphlet 3 and *Inprekorr* IV, no. 148), etc. etc. If, in spite of all this, he still upholds the same position on me, then he is doing that as a result of the actual bone of contention: he wants *to obscure* the Bolshevik conception of the party by tail-ending; and that is why he touched on everything he possibly could in his long criticism of me – except for the crucial essay in my book ('Towards a Methodology of the Problem of Organisation').

II. Dialectic of Nature

In the previous considerations again and again we came up against the problem of mediation. We were able to see how hopelessly Comrade Rudas confuses all the questions, how he is continually driven to opportunistic conclusions, because he misunderstands the decisive moment of the dialectical method. This misunderstanding – I repeat: on this point I am in full agreement with him – is in no way of a purely logical nature. The knowledge of mediations, that is those *real* forms of mediation, through which the immediate forms of appearance of society are produced, presupposes a practical–critical, a dialectical–critical standpoint *vis-à-vis* social actuality: the practical–critical standpoint of the revolutionary proletariat. The bourgeois class, even its most significant scientific representatives, sticks to the immediacy of social forms and is therefore not able to recognise society in its totality and in its becoming, that is to say, at one and the same time, as theoretically and historically dialectical. The opportunistic streams of the labour movement have sensed instinctively why they have to direct their attacks precisely against the dialectic: only by getting rid of the dialectic has it become possible for them to forget historical materialism's advance beyond the immediacy of bourgeois society, and for them to complete their ideological capitulation in the face of the bourgeoisie. The philosophical question, the overcoming of immediacy, corresponds in many respects to the earlier question, where Lenin was cited in order to present the difference between trade-union consciousness and class consciousness. For, from the standpoint of the (unovercome) immediacy of bourgeois society, the conclusions that correspond to the class position of the bourgeoisie follow of their own accord. They are nothing other than the logical (of course, in the main merely formally logical) demands of this uncritically accepted, unovercome immediate state of affairs of capitalist development.

Of course, the borders here, as everywhere, are just as fluid, and there are a whole number of mediating terms ranging from historical materialism to the theoretical forms of expression of the most superficial immediate sphere of circulation (e.g. marginal utility theory). And which real forms of mediation already exist objectively in a particular stage of development, or are present in a recognisable way is also a dialectical, i.e. a concrete, historical problem. But leaving out of the picture forms of mediation must lead to a debasement of coherent methods of knowledge: to idealism, to agnosticism, to subjectivism, etc. That is why Engels (and after him Plekhanov) emphasised distinctly that the old materialism that accepted historical appearances immediately had to become inconsistent, idealist, 'the old materialism becomes untrue to itself because it takes the ideal driving forces that operate there as ultimate causes, instead of investigating what is behind them, what are the driving forces of these driving forces. The inconsistency does not lie in the fact that *ideal* driving forces are recognised, but in the investigation not being carried further back behind these into their motive causes' (MECW 26, p. 388). Comrade Rudas fell into such idealism in his polemic against my 'idealism'. After introducing that beautiful and profound passage by Marx about the one unified science: the science of history, whose *every word* I *underwrite*, he says suddenly: 'If up until this point natural scientists have pursued natural science ahistorically, then it is much less the case today. They too are gradually realising that their science is "drumming" dialectics into them. But nature and natural scientists are two different things anyway' (*Arbeiterliteratur* XII, p. 1071). I will come back to that last sentence because it is of great significance in our difference of opinion. For the moment, though, I only want to point out the following: Comrade Rudas assumes an immanent development of the natural sciences. It is the *development of science* that drums the dialectic into the natural scientists. *Undoubtedly this also happens immediately.* The dissolution of the idealist dialectic in Germany, just like the dissolution of the Ricardo School in England and France, took place – immediately and apparently – in this fashion. It is very important to pursue the development of problems and solution separately. Marx does it, for example, magnificently in the third volume of *Theories of Surplus Value*; but in no way is he satisfied with that. Rather he points each time to the real historical process of transformation of society, which brought out as much the inner problematic of Ricardo as the crisis brought out his school. If one pursues this line of development in a purely immanent philosophical or immanent economic way, one falls of necessity into an idealistic way of seeing. For the dialectic is only in the rarest of cases *immediately* drummed in by the transformation of the material forces of production, rather this drumming in appears in the form of scientific contradictions, problems, which one tries to solve or develop, etc., scientifically, but only the materialist dialectician is in a position to recognise the 'driving forces of the driving forces', to go back to the *material* source of the emergence of the contradictions, problems, errors, the seeds of correctness, in as far as he derives their necessity from the transformation of the economic structure of society, from the class position of the thinker in question, inasmuch as he exposes that naïve immediacy that the thinker himself is caught up in as a product of social development, and, therefore, overcomes its immediacy. Marx says: 'The totality of these relations of production constitutes the economic structure of society, the real foundation, on which arises a legal and political superstructure and to which correspond definite forms of social consciousness. The mode of production of material life conditions the general process of social, political and intellectual life. It is not the consciousness of men that determines their existence, but *their social existence* that determines their consciousness' (*Preface to A Contribution to the Critique of Political Economy*, MECW 29, p. 263 – my italics).

Are the *mental forms* in which people express their relationship to nature an exception? To put it another way: do people stand in an *immediate relationship* to nature, or is their metabolic interchange with nature *mediated socially*? This is the *actual core* of my controversy with Comrades Deborin and Rudas. In what follows I will attempt to illuminate briefly the essential methodological moments of our disagreement, self-evidently without doing them the favour of representing views that they would like to think I hold, but which I have never held and on the contrary have sharply rejected.

And now I come back to the quotation cited above from Comrade Rudas's essay: 'But nature and natural scientists are two different things anyway.' Quite right. If, however, he had taken the trouble to read attentively the part of my book that he attacks, he would have found that there I talk always (on two occasions!) only of *knowledge of nature* and not nature itself (HCC, p. 24, footnote).

1. Exchange of matter with nature

If we wish to pose this question in a Marxist way, then we can only set out from the question of how the *material foundation* of our knowledge of nature is formed. Marx expressed himself quite clearly on this point in his critical presentation of Feuerbach's philosophy:

> He does not see how the sensuous world around him is, not a thing given direct from all eternity, remaining ever the same, but the product of a whole succession of generations, each standing on the shoulders of the preceding one. Feuerbach's 'conception' of the sensuous world is confined on the one hand to mere contemplation of it, and on the other to mere feeling: he stops at the abstraction 'man', never arrives at the really existing active men, and gets no further than recognising 'the true, individual, corporeal man' emotionally, i.e. he knows no other 'human relationships' 'of man to man' than love and friendship. He misses completely that the *celebrated unity of man with nature has always existed in industry*. (Italics mine)[19]

Therefore we need to investigate human productive activity.

This exchange of matter with nature appears at first as 'the ever-lasting nature-imposed condition of human existence'. Marx says of it: 'The labour process, resolved as above into its simple elementary factors, is human action with a view to the production of use values, appropriation of natural substances to human requirements; it is the necessary condition for effecting exchange of matter between man and Nature; it is the ever-lasting nature-imposed condition of human existence, and therefore is independent of every social phase of that existence, or rather, is common to every such phase' (*Capital* I, MECW 28, p. 23). In order to understand this conception correctly, concretely and dialectically, and not abstractly and formally, however, the following must be added. First, Marx is speaking here of the labour process in its simple abstract moments, so that he does not find it necessary 'to represent our labourer in connection with other labourers' (ibid.). He *is abstracting*, then, from all the social moments of the labour process, in order to work out clearly those moments that are *common to all processes of labour*. This is, as he puts it somewhere else in comments on production in general, 'a sensible abstraction in so far as it actually emphasises and defines the common aspects and thus avoids repetition' (*Contribution to the Critique of Political Economy*). At the same time, he cautions that one should not 'overlook the essential differences existing despite the unity' and points out precisely in this overlooking the 'wisdom of modern economists', a theoretical source of apologia for capitalism, as an 'eternal form' of production (ibid.). For example, immediately before the passage quoted above (*Capital* I), Marx points out expressly that the definition given here is in no way adequate for the capitalist process of production. How much this is a question of a 'sensible abstraction' is evident in the fact that here the unity of humanity is the subject and nature is the object, while in concrete observation, according to Marx 'it is moreover wrong to consider' society (an already more concrete subject than humanity) 'as a single subject, for this is a speculative approach' (*Contribution to the Critique of Political Economy*). Comrade Rudas goes further than the passage cited above in dismissing any social change. For him 'consciousness of people' is '*just as much* a natural product as the instinct of animals' (my italics). Of course I cannot object to it subjectively, if Comrade Rudas wants to clasp every donkey as a brother to his heart, and I could not take exception to it on objective grounds if he would simply say that the consciousness of people is just as much a product of nature. Of course it is a product of nature. Albeit a very *peculiar* product of nature. In the considerations on the labour process in its most simple form, cited above, Marx shows that the *material foundation* of consciousness that arises here is fundamentally different from that of animals, that is to say that the 'just as' of Comrade Rudas is – to put it mildly – un-Marxist. For already with the observation of the labour process in its simple, abstract moments 'work' is presupposed 'in a form that stamps it as exclusively human' (*Capital* I, MECW 35, p. 188). And the distinguishing characteristic is – *horribile dictu* – precisely the fact of consciousness, inasmuch as the result of the labour process was already present in the head of the worker prior to the process.

Second, this labour process is more closely defined as 'activity for the manufacture of use values', and Marx really perceives use value as 'the natural relationship between things and men', 'the existence of things for men', while exchange value – which comes along later – 'is the *social* existence of things' (*Theories of Surplus Value* III (London, 1969) p. 129). Now it is to be hoped – among Marxists – that it should not be necessary to explain thoroughly that use value and exchange value are in dialectical interaction with one another. In such a relationship the *real forms of mediation* that intervene between person and nature appear ever more diversely and decisively. Consumption, in which purely the use-value character of the thing comes to validation, is mediated and determined by forms of production in the most varied way. As Marx puts it: 'Hunger is hunger; but the hunger that is satisfied by cooked meat eaten with knife and fork differs from the hunger that devours raw meat with the help of hands, nails and teeth. Production thus produces not only the object of consumption but also the mode of consumption . . . When consumption emerges from its original primitive crudeness and immediacy – and its remaining in that state would be due to the fact that production was still primitively crude – then it is itself brought about by the object as a desire' (*Contribution to the Critique of Political Economy*, MECW 28, p. 29). And the development goes in the direction that ever more strongly emphasises the predominance of the social moment. 'In all forms in which landed property is the decisive factor, natural relations still predominate; in the forms in which the decisive factor is capital, social, historically evolved elements predominate' (ibid.).

Let us now take a look at how Marx conceives of the relationship of people to nature. Their objective mode of existence determines their consciousness of nature, that is their knowledge of nature. I will cite only a few passages:

In order to produce, they enter into definite connections and relations with one another and only within these social connections and relations does their action on nature, does production, take place. ('Wage

Labour and Capital', MECW 9, p. 211)

Production is always appropriation of nature by an individual within and
with the help of a definite social organisation. (*Contribution to the Critique of
Political Economy*, MECW 28, p. 25)

From a particular form of material production arises first of all a particular organisation of society, secondly, *a particular relationship of people to
nature. (Theories of Surplus Value* I, p. 285)

And as soon as the first animal state ceases, property (of the human) is
mediated to nature through his existence as member of a community,
family, tribe, etc., *through a [relation] to other people that determines the relation to
nature. (Theories of Surplus Value* III) (all italics mine)

I believe that these passages speak loud and clear. They say nothing
more than that which the fundamental sentence of historical materialism says: 'It is not the consciousness of men that determines their
existence, but their *social existence* that determines their consciousness.'

Our consciousness of nature, in other words our knowledge of
nature, is determined by our social being. That is what I have said in the
few observations that I have devoted to this question; nothing less, but
also nothing more. Let us look a little more closely in order to see if the
conclusion of all this is everything that my critics think can be concluded from it, or if rather the opposite is the case. Comrade Rudas
summarises his complaints in three points: (1) a dualism arises (nature:
undialectical, society: dialectical (*Arbeiterliteratur* IX, p. 501));[20] (2) the
dialectic is a human product (ibid., pp. 502–3); (3) the dialectic is 'not an
objective law, independent of the person, but a subjective law of the
person' (ibid., p. 504).[21]

The conception that Rudas represents here accommodates, [in] my
opinion, a very dangerous *subjectivism* (that is connected to Rudas's concealed and completely unvanquished Kantianism). For him, namely, in
all circumstances – as for Comrade Deborin in the passage quoted at the
beginning – it appears that subject = person (society); object = nature.
From this follows of course that everything that is a product of 'people'

(i.e. of the social-historical process of development) falls on the side of the subject and a true objectivity is achieved only by those things and connections that not only merely exist independently of people (independently of the subject of knowledge), which is the correct Marxist understanding, but are also independent of the historical process of development of society. I will address shortly the question of the extent to which the dialectic is a 'human product' in my conception. But for the moment I must draw clear attention to the way that Rudas (and obviously Deborin who is at one with him on this matter) conceives the opposition of subject and object undialectically, inflexibly. For them – as for Kant and all Kantians – on the one side stands the subject and on the other side the object, and only that which is free from any contact with the subject can be objective. This conception differs only in the way it is formulated from that of the neo-Kantians, e.g. Rickert, where subject is that which can never be object (*Gegenstand der Erkenntnis*, 3rd edition). Rudas's conception is not only in its undialectical foundation close to the Kantian one, but it also takes as its starting point a similar 'epistemological' problematic, in so far as it does not seek the question of objectivity in the real historical interaction of objective and subjective moments of development, in order to analyse it in its living interaction. Rather from the outset (*a priori*, timelessly in epistemological terms) it attempts to purify 'objectivity' of 'all subjective ingredients'. Neither Rudas nor Deborin pursues the logic of his position through to the end. For they would have to place *all* social forms of appearance on the side of subjectivity and deny that the criterion of objectivity – the independence of the existence of objects from the knowing, experiencing, etc., subject – exists in society. Of course they shrink away from such conclusions which refute the ABC of Marxism. But whoever thinks through fully the citations introduced here would have to reach the conclusion that anything that is 'the work of people' is 'subjective'. Given that we know that human beings make their own history – history must be a field of subjectivism.

That is self-evidently nonsense. Let us presuppose that I do maintain (I will show in a moment that it is actually the opposite case) that the dialectic is a product of historical development. Even in this case the dialectic would not be a 'subjective' thing. Land rent, capital, profit, etc., are nothing but products of this development and yet who would claim that they are merely subjective things? Only he who is caught up in the immediate perception of bourgeois society and yet wants to reach beyond it, who recognises the 'subjective' moment in social conditions, but is incapable of recognising at the same time the dialectical mutual interaction of subjectivity and objectivity in them, is not in a position to grasp the type and basis of their objectivity. (Cf. Marx's critique of Ricardo's radical pupil, who began to see through the commodity fetish, but saw in it something purely subjective.) Comrade Rudas, who – when he makes 'epistemological' observations – is forced to such conclusions, plunges, out of understandable fear, into the mechanically and diametrically opposed extreme in his historical analyses. As we have shown, he perceives social development as a process cleansed of 'any subjective ingredient'. He has a mechanical and Kantian conception of objective reality.

So, the dialectic would not be a subjective thing, if it were a product of the economic and historical development of humanity. (Comrade Rudas would appear to understand objective as meaning the opposite of socially determined. Therefore he speaks of the 'objective process of production' in contrast to its 'capitalist husk', which obviously represents something subjective for Rudas (*Arbeiterliteratur* IX, pp. 515–16).)[22] Clearly according to my conception, it is no such thing. The 'conundrums' that Comrade Rudas poses (ibid., p. 502)[23] are very easy to answer. Self-evidently society arose *from* nature. Self-evidently nature and its laws existed *before* society (that is to say before humans). Self-evidently the dialectic *could* not possibly be effective as an *objective principle of development* of society, if it were not already effective as a principle of development of nature before society, if it did not already *objectively exist*. From that, however, follows neither that social development could produce no new, equally objective forms of movement, dialectical moments, nor that the dialectical moments in the development of nature would be *knowable* without the mediation of these new social dialectical forms. For obviously we can speak only about those moments of the dialectic that we already know or are on the point of knowing. The dialectical conception of knowledge as a process does not only include the possibility that in the course of history we get to know new contents, new objects, that we have not known until now. It also means that new contents can emerge, which can be understood only with the aid of principles of knowledge that are just as newly available. We are aware that at this very moment we know only one part of infinite objective reality (and that part quite certainly is known only partially correctly). But in understanding the process of knowledge dialectically, as a process, we must also understand this process as, at the same time, *part* of the objective social process of development. That is to say, we must understand that the *what*, the *how*, the *how far*, etc., of our knowledge is determined by the stage of development of the objective process of development of society. In so far as we grasp the dialectical character of knowledge, we understand it simultaneously as a *historical process*. As a historical process, knowledge is only one part, only the conscious (correctly or falsely conscious) part of the historical process of development of that uninterrupted transformation of social being, which occurs likewise in uninterrupted interaction with nature (exchange of matter between society and nature).

This exchange of matter with nature cannot possibly be achieved – even on the most primitive level – without possessing a certain degree of objectively correct knowledge about the processes of nature (which exist prior to people and function independently of them). The most primitive Negro village could not exist for a day if its inhabitants could not observe and predict correctly, to a certain degree, the appearances of nature that are important to them (that is to say, in their objectivity which is independent of people). Of course these observations are restricted to a small circle of natural appearances; of course the 'theories' whereby the meaning of the appearance is made conscious are naïve, wrong or even a conscious deception. However, here too, given the imperative of existing in objective reality, there exists, at the same time, the need – as far as possible – to know it correctly in its objectivity. The type and degree of this knowledge depend on the economic structure of society. For the type and degree of the exchange of matter between society and nature, the material foundation of knowledge, depends on the stage of development of the economic structure of society.

At countless points, Marx emphasises expressly that human knowledge is determined according to its source, according to the problems before which it is placed and which have to be solved under threat of decline of the society concerned, i.e. it is determined by the economic conditions of life of the society, on which basis the particular knowledge arises. I will point only to the example of the periods of the Nile movements as the origin of Egyptian astronomy (*Capital* I). But the question is: are also the categories in which objective reality is summarised for human knowledge at any one time determined by the economic structure, by social being? It seems to me to be indubitable that this alone must be what Marx meant. Probably nobody would argue against this in the case of conceptions of nature in pre-capitalist societies; but that Marx also thought this of the knowledge of nature in his own time is demonstrated in a passage from a letter about Darwin, whom he held in high esteem, and whose theories he always considered to be fundamental. He writes to Engels:

> It is curious how Darwin recognises in animals and plants his English society with its division of labour, competition, search for new markets, 'inventions' and Malthus's 'fight for existence'. It is Hobbes's 'bellum omnium contra omnes', and it reminds one of Hegel in the *Phenomenology*, where bourgeois society features as a 'spiritual animal kingdom', while in Darwin the animal kingdom features as bourgeois society. (MECW 41, p. 381)

It would appear to be quite obvious to reproach such a conception with relativism or agnosticism. However, with what justification? Relativism would arise if the social-historical conditionedness of human thought were to be conceived in an undialectical, bourgeois way, i.e. either in an abstract, formal way or atheoretically and in a historicist manner (e.g. *à la* Ranke). Relativism would arise if one were to argue that the conception of nature in the Negro village and in capitalist society are both determined by the economic structure of their social being, and so therefore it follows that both are equally as close to (i.e. equidistant from) objective truth. For the Marxist, however, the material basis of knowledge (here exchange of matter between society and nature) is a concrete and objective process, and that means that it is a historical process which is knowable with theory. The consequence of this is that in this process particular directions, particular stages, etc., can be observed. And these stages are neither of equal ranking (as for historicism) in relation to the objective knowledge reached at any one time, nor is the temporally later stage necessarily the higher one in every respect, because the development is supposed to go in a straight line upwards (evolutionism). It is rather more likely that concrete analysis of the economic structure of society at any one time determines the stage of development of the exchange of matter between society and nature. And from that results the stage of development (height, intensity, type, etc.) of the knowledge of nature. The knowledge achieved at any one time is relative only in as far as it can be modified, indeed can be proven false, through a higher development of the economic structure of society (and a corresponding expansion, greater intensity, etc., of the exchange of matter between society and nature). However – in as far as it pertains to the objective reality of social being and the nature mediated through this – it is objective truth, absolute truth, which only changes its position, its theoretical explanation, etc., because of the knowledge that 'overcomes' it, and which is more comprehensive and more correct. (As for example the correct observations of Ptolemaic astronomy or Tycho de Brache's astronomy are 'overcome' in Copernican astronomy. They remain objective truths although the theories devised to explain them have proven to be incorrect.) Dialectical materialism contains 'relativism' to the extent that the dialectician must be conscious that the categories in which he conceives objective reality (society and nature) are determined by the social being of his present moment, that they are only mental summations of this objective reality. (Categories are 'forms of existence, conditions of existence' – Marx.) Historical materialism eclipses all the methods that went before it, on the one hand, inasmuch as it conceives reality as a whole consistently as a *historical process*, and on the other hand, inasmuch as it is in a position to understand the starting point of knowledge at any one time. Knowledge itself is understood to be just as much a product of the objective process of history. It is not compelled to absolutise either the knowledge itself, or the present historical reality which determines the form and content of knowledge (as Hegel was still compelled to do). If one wishes to call such clarity about the foundations and concrete determinations of knowledge relativism or agnosticism – one can do so, but it is a bourgeois misuse of terminology.

For what my critics call my agnosticism is nothing other than my denial that there is a socially unmediated, i.e. an immediate relationship of humans to nature in the present stage of social development – self-evidently I reject getting into disputes over utopian future possibilities. Therefore, I am of the opinion that our knowledge of nature is socially mediated, because its material foundation is socially mediated; and so I remain true to the Marxian formulation of the method of historical materialism: 'it is social being that determines consciousness'. How a dualism (a dualism of nature and society) is supposed to arise out of this conception is unfathomable for me. If one – as Deborin and Rudas quite obviously do – holds on to the possibility of an immediate relationship to nature, then according to this understanding the knowledge of nature and society develop alongside each other, independently from each other, *dualistically*. Inasmuch as this dualism is overcome, it happens through the extinguishing of all specific social-historical categories and only those categories can be used for the knowledge of history that can also be used in natural science. We were able to admire where all this leads us in Rudas's tailist theory of class consciousness and we will be able to appreciate it in Deborin in what follows. And if, accordingly, the reason for the transformation of our knowledge of nature is not sought in the transformation of social being (which always changes the type and degree, etc., of the exchange of matter with nature), then either pure idealism ensues, as with Comrade Rudas and his immanent-dialectical development of science, or it must be accepted that the fundamental changes in natural science at any one time are reflections of changes in nature. (Along the lines of – the sun used to circle around the earth, but now the relationship has reversed itself – and so Copernicus is explained; but we do not want to go any further with this nonsense.) Just how far Comrade Rudas is from even perceiving the problem, just how much he tries to hide his undialectical mode of thinking through hysterical outcries about idealism, dualism, etc., is displayed in the following passage from his polemic. As decisive characteristics of the dialectical method I emphasised (HCC, p. 24): 'the historical changes in the reality underlying the categories as the root cause of the changes in thought'. Comrade Rudas says: 'What this philosophical thieves' Latin means is utterly irrelevant for us here, for it suffices to decipher that "a change in thought is the matter under discussion". Only people can think, and that suffices completely for our purposes' (*Arbeiterliteratur* IX, p. 503). It would appear that the mere mention of a 'change in thought' is enough to awaken the noble indignation of Comrade Rudas, and in his noble indignation he does not even notice that the vilified 'change of thought' is seen here as an effect, indeed as an effect of the objective reality that exists outside the thought (the reality underlying the categories). Thus the sentence means that a change in material (the reality that underlies thought) must take place, in order that a change in thought may follow. It might be an unpleasant fact for Comrade Rudas that humans are necessary for *thought*, that in their heads reality takes on a conscious form, for he obviously as much wishes to eliminate human activity from politics as he hopes to eliminate the human process of thought from thought, but it cannot be changed. That objective dialectics are in reality independent of humans and were there before the emergence of people, is precisely what was *asserted* in this passage; but that for *thinking the dialectic*, for the dialectic as knowledge (and that and that *alone* was addressed in the remark), thinking people are necessary. This might be doubted only by Comrade Rudas who makes of the dialectical objectivity of thinking a bourgeois-logicistic objectivism and whose eclectic thought is haunted by reminiscences of the Bolzano–Husserlesque 'sentence in itself', hints of a truth that is independent of any being thought.

The dualism of my conception appears somewhat doubtful. It is precisely according to my – and only my – interpretation of Marxism that our knowledge as a *whole* has a uniform source: the development of society and the exchange of matter between society and nature, which develops in accord with this development. Every conception that disputes this, assuming an immediate relationship, i.e. a relationship of human to nature that is independent of social being (as source of knowledge of nature), must imagine both these realms of knowledge developing independently of each other; *that is dualistically*; and must assume the common principle, the dialectic, if it is yet found, to be merely a principle of knowledge, a type of higher logic. That is to say it *becomes idealistic.*

2. Simple and higher categories of the dialectic

Of course this interconnection is not in any way a mechanical dependence of both realms of cognition on each other. Since its material foundation is a dialectical process, since the economic structure of society and exchange of matter with nature permanently find themselves in a real dialectical interaction with one another, the objective interconnection is also always a dialectical one. Even within social phenomena these interconnections do not simply form, but are formed in a way that changes in the course of historical development. That is in a way whereby not only the phenomena change their contents – such changes are recognised by bourgeois history-writing too – but also the structure of the interconnection changes as a result of the changes of real materials. Thus Marx points out repeatedly such an 'unequal development of material production and, e.g. that of art' (*A Contribution to the Critique of Political Economy*, MECW 28, p. 46). The following expositions, however, show that art is really only an example, and the same unequal development can emerge between law and production. An insoluble problem ensues only for mechanical bourgeois thought – which has to remain trapped in the fetishistic antinomy of 'eternal iron laws' or 'unique individuality'. In dialectical materialism the structural problem is solved historically (i.e. through pointing out the concrete, real historical genesis of the structure concerned), and the historical problem is solved theoretically (that is through pointing out the obedience to the law that the concrete material under consideration has produced). Therefore Marx stresses the following in relation to the sequence of economic categories: 'their order of succession is determined by their mutual relationship in modern bourgeois society and this is quite the reverse of what appears to be natural to them or in accordance with the sequence of historical development' (MECW 28, p. 44).

However, in no way does the fact that the real objective process is dialectical and that the emergence and linkages of the insights that correctly reflect it are also dialectical mean that all knowledge always appears in the *form of knowledge of the dialectical method*. The claim of the young Marx: 'Reason has always existed, just not always in reasonable form' is also true of the dialectic. It depends on the economic structure of society and the class position that the perceiver takes up within it whether and how far an objective dialectical interconnection adopts a dialectical form in thought, whether and how much people *can* become conscious of the dialectical character of the interconnection concerned. Under some circumstances it may not come to light at all in thought, epistemologically. It might appear as an insoluble contradiction, as an antinomy. It might be understood correctly in terms of some of its traits, without it being possible to determine its correct place in the development as a whole, etc. From what has been said so far it is clear that such knowledge can be, despite all that, at least partially, objectively correct. But theoretically correct, dialectical, knowledge can be found only when the historical development of society is so advanced that the real problems that lie at the basis of these contradictions, etc., are solved historically, or advance towards their solution. In other words: the dissolution, the overcoming of dialectical contradiction is produced by reality through real historical processes. Thought can, under particular conditions, pre-empt such processes mentally; however that is only when this overcoming is present as a real, if practically immature, tendency of development objectively in the real process of history. And if this interconnection has not become fully conscious through the real process of history, if each dialectical problem is not related to its concrete material basis, then that mental pre-empting must stray into abstraction, into idealism (Hegel).

At this point the most serious objection to my conception of dialectics, raised by Deborin, can be appreciated: my neglect of the simple categories of the dialectic in favour of the higher ones. Deborin says: 'We simply wish to underline the fact that Hegel always considered the process of development in all its moments, that, scaling the peak of the absolute idea, he showed at the same time that the process as a whole forms its content. The forwards movement begins from abstract and simple concepts or categories and advances to the next concepts, which become increasingly richer and more concrete' (*Arbeiterliteratur* IX, p. 636). As a description of the *mode of exposition* of Hegel that is – by and large – correct, and it is possible that Hegel as an idealist was often trapped in the illusion that this mode of exposition of the dialectical categories corresponded as much to their objective real interconnections as to the real process of their discernibility. For Marx, to whom Deborin 'by and large' ascribes this point of view (ibid.), it is certainly not the case. Marx was always completely clear about the fact that what is lower (simpler, more abstract) can only be *recognised from* the higher (more complicated, more concrete). He says: 'The anatomy of man is a key to the anatomy of the ape. On the other hand, rudiments of more advanced forms in the lower species of animals can only be understood when the more advanced forms are already known. Bourgeois economy thus provides a key to the economy of antiquity, etc.' (*A Contribution to the Critique of Political Economy*, MECW 28, p. 42). The simple category is then, for Marx, the starting point of the *exposition* (commodity, labour, money, etc.). His materialist dialectic, his historical materialism, however, saves him from the error of overlooking the historical (under certain circumstances historically delayed, much diverted) character of simple categories. He comments there precisely about labour: 'Labour seems to be a very simple category. The notion of labour in this universal form, as labour in general, is also extremely old. Nevertheless "labour" in this simplicity is economically considered just as modern a category as the relations that give rise to this simple abstraction. . . . The simplest abstraction, which plays a decisive role in modern political economy, an abstraction that expresses an ancient relation existing in all social formations, nevertheless appears to be actually true in this abstract form only as a category of the most modern society' (*A Contribution to the Critique of Political Economy*, MECW 28, p. 40). Therefore: 'the method of advancing from the abstract to the concrete is thinking the way in which thinking assimilates the concrete and reproduces it as a concrete mental category. This is, however, by no means the process of the evolution of the concrete world itself' (ibid.). If he identifies the method of Hegel 'by and large' with that of Marx, Deborin succumbs to Hegel's illusion that 'the real world is the result of thinking which causes its own synthesis, its own deepening and its own movement' (ibid.). It would not be too difficult to derive this method from all of Marx's later, concrete explanations; and thereby one could discern that he always refused to conceive the concrete totality as constructed in reality of its simple abstract elements, although he (very correctly!) often used this construction as a mode of exposition. I will cite only one passage about crises:

> No crisis can exist unless sale and purchase are separated from one another and come into conflict, or the contradictions contained in money as a means of payment actually come into play; crisis, therefore, cannot exist without manifesting itself at the same time in its simple form, as the contradiction between sale and purchase and the contradiction of money as a means of payment. But these are merely *forms*, general possibilities of crisis, and hence also forms, abstract forms, of actual crisis. In them, the nature of crisis appears in its simplest forms, and, in so far as this form is itself the simplest content of crisis, in its simplest content. But the content is not yet *substantiated*. Simple circulation of money and even the circulation of money as a means of payment – and both come into being long *before* capitalist production, while there are no crises – are possible and actually take place without crises. These forms alone, therefore, do not explain why their crucial aspect becomes prominent and why the potential contradiction contained in them becomes a real contradiction. (*Theories of Surplus Value* II, p. 512)

It is quite easy to see in all this the interconnection of 'simple' and 'higher' categories in Marx. Higher categories must be produced in reality by the historical process, and they must be correctly recognised in their dialectical interconnections, so that the historical and systematic functions of the simple categories that correspond to them can be recognised. To imagine the process the other way round is an idealist illusion and leads – if carried to a logical conclusion – to an apologia for what exists, whereby the simple category figures as a fundamental element, which Marx convincingly refutes in the passage just cited on bourgeois crisis theory. I would like to remark in passing that the much mentioned 'contradictions' between the first and the third volumes of *Capital* – the inability of bourgeois economy to understand that the more concrete, modifying determinations of the third volume *must* have been known to Marx before the writing of the first volume – can be traced back to a similar methodological disposition. Clarity about this aspect of Marx's method is of great importance in understanding the materialist dialectic. There must be clarity about the fact that the so-called simple categories are not trans-historical elements of the system, but are *just as much* products of historical development as the concrete totalities to which they belong, and that, therefore, simple categories are correctly grasped from higher, more complicated, more concrete ones. That is to say it is only the comprehension of the concrete whole, to which the simple categories belong, that makes possible knowledge of the simple ones and not the other way round, even if – as has already been outlined – its exposition must often take a reversed path.

All this provides an answer to Rudas's question – about whose rationale he does not even dare 'express his suspicions' (*Arbeiterliteratur* IX, p. 503) – as to why precisely I characterise as the decisive dialectical categories not transformation of quantity into quality, etc., but rather interaction of subject and object, unity of theory and praxis, alteration of the categories as effect of the change of material (reality underlying the categories). It is because, Comrade Rudas, expressed in thought in these categories is what is specific and new in that social stage of development when the proletariat emerges as an independent class and sets about the transformation of society. It would contradict the essence of historical materialism if we did not conceive the emergence of the dialectical method as just as much a part of the real historical process, perceiving simply a scientific development as much in the idealistic dialectic of Hegel as in its overturning, its 'putting on its feet' by Marx. We must always keep in view those real economic, class-conditioned moments of history that make this mental development possible and motivated it. Then it becomes clear how much, on the one hand, those categories that in Hegel himself, in the most abstract and idealist part of his *Logic* ('Logic of the Concept') form the peak of his system, become real, practical moments of the proletarian class struggle. And, on the other hand, the 'simple' categories, whose determination and discernibility is dependent in both cases on the 'higher' categories, lose their idealist character in Marx, are placed on their feet, and appear as abstractions motivated by the historical process of development. Whatever 'simple' categories one takes in Marx, one will find that they can be correctly grasped only from this perspective. Whoever allows the 'decisive' categories mentioned above to disappear from the system – as do all opportunists – eternalises the 'simple' categories in the form that they adopt in bourgeois immediacy. Thereby any dialectical function is gradually lost. Such a 'Marxist' economics all of a sudden transforms itself into vulgar bourgeois economics (Kautsky, Hilferding, etc.). 'Dialectical' categories that have been severed from this connection can even be used by bourgeois researchers; it is not inconceivable that they might, for example, be able to work with the transformation of quantity into quality. The category becomes properly dialectical only in the *context of the dialectical totality*, which can be achieved – mentally – only through the dialectical mediation of the 'simple' categories with the concrete 'higher' ones. It has to be in this interconnection because only this connection offers the real and correct *mental reproduction of the real historical process*. It is therefore social being that determines the consciousness of humans.

3. Once again: exchange of matter with nature

And their consciousness of nature too. It would not only be a narrow and inflexible conception, but also a dualistic one that did not consider our real relationship to nature, the material basis of our knowledge of nature, by starting out from our exchange of matter with nature, and did not consider this exchange of matter with nature in its *double determination*, as much as an interaction with nature – which exists independently from humans – as well as simultaneously determined by the economic structure of society at any one time. I repeat: every Marxist with correct instincts would adopt this standpoint in talking about the astronomy of the Egyptians, or the physics of Aristotle. Does modern natural science adopt a special place, then? Is this dialectical double determination not valid for it too?

Of course, if we answer this question with a 'no', we have to say no in a *dialectical way*. This means that we must always be clear that modern natural science does indeed adopt a special place in the history of human knowledge of nature. And that it is in no way appropriate, indeed it would clearly be a false relativism, if we treated it mechanically, in the same way as the knowledge of nature of past epochs. (Here, for example, is where Duhau's mistake lies.) However, is it not the case that capitalist society, whose exchange of matter with nature forms the material basis of modern natural science, likewise adopts a special place in the social process of development? Is its position as the last class society only quantitatively, only positionally, defined as 'last', only in comparison with earlier class societies? Certainly not. Here indeed quantity transforms into quality: the most highly developed class society produces the material, economic and social preconditions for socialism. It prepares the end of the prehistory of humanity. Socialist society is, for example, the inheritor of all the tremendous achievements that capitalism has brought about in the field of technology. And this inheritance distinguishes itself essentially from the way that it itself adopted the heritage of the Middle Ages in its time. For the elements of technology that early capitalism took from feudalism in decline did not compose among themselves in any way such a unified connection as the technology of our epoch. They only really linked together through being taken over into capitalist production, while socialism, if it is not only to develop further the technology that it takes over, but also to transform it internally, raising it to a higher level (for example, by the revolutionising of the capitalist division of labour), must first of all, and perhaps over a long period of transition, be compelled to work with the technical achievements of capitalism that have been adopted (and of course further developed). The real economic determinations that make possible comprehension of the economic structure of society and the true driving forces of its history (in pre-capitalist times as well) appear only with the development of capitalism. Those elements of knowledge, those 'simple' categories of the economy that make possible scientific knowledge of society and history are, as 'forms of being, conditions of existence', in part, products of capitalist development (labour *per se*), in part, only in capitalism do they accrue a function in the economy as a whole, whereby they can be understood as elements of the system as a whole (money). Capitalist society is not simply a particular historical phase of humanity's development, but one in which the driving forces of this development clearly emerge into correct discernibility – of course, only once its self-criticism, fulfilled in the theory and praxis of the proletariat, is just as clearly evident (*A Contribution to the Critique of Political Economy*).

This development of the relations of production, which presupposes a corresponding development of the productive forces, must go hand in hand with a corresponding development of the exchange of matter between society and nature. Indeed, capitalist development produces the material preconditions for socialism (technology, machines, etc., Lenin on electrification). The command over natural forces reaches, indeed to an ever increasing extent, an expansive intensity and system, which would be unthinkable for previous societies. Knowledge of nature develops in uninterrupted interaction with this process: it arises on the basis of this social being, it is its product, and, at the same time, it is one of the most effective vehicles for abetting this process. (Since I may count on little sympathy for dialectical interconnection among Comrades Rudas and Deborin, I will once again stress the following: that the modern natural sciences are a product of capitalist development does not mean that they are something 'subjective'. For a start, capitalist society is itself an 'objective' thing; second, it makes possible an adequate, objective, systematic knowledge of nature – in previously unsuspected ways. Indeed such an adequate, objective and systematic knowledge of nature is, to a much greater degree and in a far broader arena, etc., than for earlier forms of society, a condition of existence for capitalism. Capitalism does not only make this knowledge possible, but it makes it possible because it is a necessity for it.) So, the fact that modern natural science is a product of capitalist society takes nothing away from its objectivity. Indeed a thorough and concrete analysis of the relationship of this science to its material basis, to the exchange of matter between capitalist society and nature, could point out why the modes of knowledge of previous societies, modes that were infused by mythological forms, had to be liquidated, and why a natural science that was in a qualitatively higher degree objective could arise only on the basis of capitalism.

Here two questions arise immediately – both closely connected to each other and central to this controversy. First: is modern knowledge of nature conditioned by the social being of capitalism only in the fact of it being produced by it? Is it otherwise (in its construction, in its categories, in its method, etc.) entirely independent of this social being? Second: does the objectivity of an insight mean that it must be dialectical under all circumstances? The first question has already been answered above. To say yes to it would mean – contra Marx – the assumption of a socially unmediated relationship to nature. It would mean assuming that the natural scientist, in so far as he pursues pure natural science, stands outside of society, and that the categories of social development (forms of being, conditions of existence!) exert no influence on the process of knowledge that is taking place in his head. If we assumed all that, we would have fallen into the same sort of primitive and mechanically causal, undialectical mode of speculation, for which bourgeois science likes to reproach historical materialism, when it ascribes to it knowledge of 'economy' as a special 'sphere' that immediately and causally determines the other spheres (law, art, etc.), only then indignantly to reject this – self-invented – causal connection. If, however, one perceives in the economy, with Marx, 'the anatomy of civil society', then one has to say that there is no manifestation of life in bourgeois society that can exist without a relationship to this anatomy and which would be knowable independently of it. There is no manifestation that could not and would not have to be explained by this anatomy, as much on the part of the subject (categories as forms of existence of the subject in *all* manifestations of life), as on the part of the object (social determinedness of the exchange of matter between society and nature).

Here, however, the concretising of the problem comes up against a factual historical obstacle, which is admittedly well suited to illuminating more closely the methodological side of the question. We pointed earlier to Marx's assertion that historical knowledge depends on the self-criticism of a society, on insight into the material foundations of its existence and the knowledge that has grown on its basis. In this respect, the transition from pre-capitalist forms of society to capitalism is markedly different to the transition from capitalism to socialism. In the former case the transition was immediate, vast, and in a most conspicuous way a transformation of the exchange of matter between society and nature. Indeed so much so that the transition was apparent in the various types of transformation of knowledge of nature earlier than it was apparent in society. (Without a doubt the struggle over Copernican astronomy is simultaneously an ideological form of class struggle.) In contrast to this, it appears that in the transition of capitalism to socialism the exchange of matter between society and nature remains unchanged at first, indeed it appears as if its previous lines of development even temporarily experience intensification. The prospect of transformation in this area too takes place only with the second stage of communism (overturning of the capitalist division of labour, abolition of the difference between mental and manual labour, transformation of the relationship between town and country). Of course here the transition is, as everywhere, a fluid one. It can only be a question of the predominance of one moment, not the exclusion of the other. It is altogether possible that the present crisis of the natural sciences is already a sign of the imminent revolutionising of its material basis and not merely a reflex of the general ideological crisis of capitalism in decline.

However, as long as we are not in a position to demonstrate concretely the historical genesis of the emergence of our perceptions out of their material basis, i.e. not only *that* they are, but *what* they are, and *how*, etc., as Marx accomplished for our socio-historical perceptions, our mode of looking is lacking an important *objective* moment of the dialectic: history. In no way do I want to deny that the natural sciences contain elements of historical cognition. I do not deny that the first steps of the 'unified science of history' demanded by Marx (Kant–Laplace, Darwin, etc.) is contained in them. Even pre-Marxist knowledge of society contains historical elements (Steuart, Hegel, French historians, etc.). But truly historical and dialectical knowledge appears only in Marx. It emerges only through dialectical knowledge of the present as a moment of the total process. I suppose that nobody would maintain that these historical elements stand in the centre of modern natural science's set of questions, or that precisely the most developed natural sciences and the other methodologically exemplary natural sciences would consciously wrestle with these questions. For these questions to be important, it would be requisite, on the one hand, to be clear about the epoch or periods that match certain insights, because they capture specific, historical objective and real relationships in thought, and, on the other hand, it would be requisite to understand dialectically the necessary emergence of insights from the objective, real process of history (Engels speaks clearly about economic insights in his first claim in the letter to F.A. Lange – *Neue Zeit* XXVIII, I, p. 185). To what extent all knowledge of nature can ever be transformed into historical knowledge, that is to say whether there are material actualities in nature that never change their structure, or only over such large periods of time that they do not feature as changes for human knowledge, cannot be raised here because even where it seems to us that historical developments have occurred their historical character can now be grasped only to a very small extent. This means that we have got as far as recognising that the history of humanity *must* be preceded by an *objective* development of history that covers an unending span of time, yet the real links of mediation between this and our history are known by us only in small part, or indeed, in some areas, not at all. And that is not because there is insufficient material available to us today, or because of the present under-development of our research methods (many natural sciences tower above the sciences of history when it comes to precision). It is because the capacity to discover the material foundations of knowledge, and to derive knowledge from this material basis dialectically, has not yet up until this point been produced by objective real developments. The good old natural scientists are as dogmatically impartial *vis-à-vis* nature as Ricardo was *vis-à-vis* capitalist society. (The bad ones are eaten up by scepticism and can be considered here only as a symptom of the crisis.) This does not hinder them at all – as the example of Ricardo shows – in reaching objectively correct knowledge. Ricardo attained it as well in many areas. But it does make it impossible for them to interpret the contradictions that arise in concrete material as dialectical contradictions, and to classify the individual moments, as shown earlier, both theoretically and historically, in their connection to the totality, as moments of a unified historical process. Such a historical turn in the natural sciences, a growing insight into its own origin (awareness of its geocentric character) would make it as little 'relativistic' as social science has become as a result of its Marxist insight into the real genesis of its own knowledge. On the contrary.

4. For us and for itself

And now we have arrived at the crux of my objections to some of Friedrich Engels's statements. (I have no intention of entering into the corrupt demagoguery of Deborin and Rudas, who claim that I want *really* to play Marx off against Engels. I mean what I have said and I say it here unambiguously so that nobody can accuse me of 'diplomacy'.) It pertains to the famous passage on the 'thing-in-itself' in *Feuerbach* (MECW 26, p. 367). Comrade Rudas reproaches my 'pedantic, philological, school-masterly precision' (*Arbeiterliteratur* IX, p. 509) because I counter Engels's opposition of in-itself and for-us with the claim that these two concepts are not oppositions but correlates, and that the dialectical opposite of in-itself is for-itself (HCC, pp. 131–3). In any case, Rudas corrects himself straight away: establishing this opposition is not simply pedantry on my part, but rather a case of my orthodox Hegelianism coming to light. Poor Hegel – he has to be blamed for everything that Rudas's opportunistically distorted 'Marxism', his 'repressed' neo-Kantianism, is unable to grasp. At one point, he lays the foundation for the dualism of nature and history, and at another point he hopes that alizarin reaches the for-itself stage and recognises itself as an object.[24] It is, as Marx said of Dietzgen (who otherwise does not deserve this comparison with Rudas), a pity that Comrade Rudas 'has not studied Hegel'. Neither for Hegel, nor for the 'orthodox Hegelians', is it a case of alizarin recognising itself as an object, of it reaching the for-itself stage. But rather that precisely the difference between our insights into nature and into history (which, as we have seen, Deborin strongly underwrites), rests on the fact that for history the object, material itself, pushes towards being for-itself (and therefore makes possible knowledge in the form of the for-itself), while knowledge of nature is played out in the form of the correlate in-itself – for-us. Hegel's limitation, which, despite his occasional great realism, pushed him towards a mythological idealism, is that he did not care to demonstrate this for-itself, this object that recognises itself in its material concreteness, in its historical becoming, and in its having become, and this was simply because it did not really exist in his time, because people's social being really determines their consciousness. We cannot go any further here into the problem of the construction of the system in Hegel. But we just had to, on the one hand, transfer the fantastic nonsense that Comrade Rudas attributes to Hegel on to Comrade Rudas's account, and on the other hand, point out that the in-itself – for-us – for-itself indicates real as well as mental mediations, and that the for-us means something different in a [system] where these mediations are missing. I turn your attention to what has already been said about the relationship of simple and higher categories, and now return to the passage in Engels.

Engels says: 'The most telling refutation of this as of all other philosophical crotchets is praxis, namely experiment and industry.' The thing-in-itself is turned into a thing-for-us by experiment and industry. This last remark is without doubt correct, and has never been doubted by me. But what I question, simply, is whether philosophical crotchets are really refuted thereby. Without here going properly into the question of to what extent Engels misunderstands Kant, I must preface my comments with a few remarks. It is not enough just to say that Kant's philosophy in general is agnostic; rather one has to ask where and to what extent it is agnostic. And second (and precisely this question is closely connected to the last one), to what extent is Kant's agnosticism refuted by Engels's arguments? If it were just a matter of the undiscernibility of the external world in Kant, or the subjective character of the appearance of knowledge (as with the Greek Sophists like Gorgias or the subjective idealists such as Berkeley), then this would be a truly convincing refutation. But, as Franz Mehring has already noted, this is not the case with Kant. Mehring says on exactly this point: 'And yet we must mention it because Engels actually did Kant an injustice, in seeking to deal with his theory of knowledge as a "philosophical crotchet". It is true that Kant says things are not seen as they are, but rather as they appear to our senses, but he did not draw from this the conclusion that the world of appearance is a mere illusion, but rather a world of practical experience, so that indeed he too would have underwritten the sentence with which Engels seeks to refute him: the proof of the pudding is in the eating' (*Neue Zeit* XXVIII, I, p. 176; similarly various passages of my book, e.g. p. 199). Comrade Rudas also senses the weakness of his position, in admitting 'that Kant maintained the complete discernibility of the world of appearances. But precisely because of

that he was a *half*-materialist' (*Arbeiterliteratur* IX, p. 510). Two observations are necessary here. First, that for Kant 'appearance' means
something *objective*, not an illusion (cf. on this point *Prolegomena*, part 1,
footnote III, the polemic against Berkeley). In this respect he is certainly
a precursor of Hegel – if a very incomplete one, incomplete because he
is not in a position to grasp dialectically the contradiction that lies in the
objectivity of 'appearance', and is first worked out clearly by Hegel (in
the 'logic of essence'). Second, that this 'half-materialism' of Kant, the
restriction of human knowledge to 'appearances', the undiscernibility
of the thing-in-itself, was also shared by the materialists of the eighteenth century. I will simply call upon a witness who is unlikely to be
charged with idealism, Plekhanov. He quotes Holbach: 'Humans are
not supposed to know everything. Humans are not supposed to penetrate into the essence of things, nor to reach first principles' (*Beiträge zur
Geschichte des Materialismus*). And in a polemical passage against Lange,
who sees in Robinet a precursor of Kant because he alleged the undiscernibility of the thing-in-itself, he says: 'But Robinet says of the
thing-in-itself only that which Holbach and Helvetius say' (ibid.), etc.
Self-evidently a contradiction is contained in all these positions; self-evidently all these thinkers, if they aim to get beyond this limit, leave
behind the materialist or half-materialist perspective of their philosophy and fall victim to agnosticism or idealism (or both in the case of
Kant).

Consequently, the crucial point is, on the one hand, the question of
how far the world of 'appearances' is objective, and how far it is merely
subjective; and, on the other hand, what the undiscernibility of the
thing-in-itself means for the objectivity of knowledge. We have already
pointed out that Kant rejects the thoroughgoing subjectivism of
Berkeley, indeed he even labels it a 'scandal of reason'; but, at the same
time, we pointed out that thereby he arrives at a contradictory philosophical position. For on the one hand, he must understand the forms of
the 'world of appearance' as subjective, as produced by the subject of
knowledge, and in Kant that is, of course, not the individual knowing
subject. On the other hand, the content, the material of this knowledge,
what Kant calls sensibility, is completely independent of the subject; it is
caused by the 'affection' of the subject by the thing-in-itself. Knowledge,

then, is possible only as a result of this affection by the thing-in-itself (as is well known, Kant argues against the possibility of a knowledge whose material is not sensible), but human knowledge of the thing-in-itself is completely unattainable, transcendent. (Plekhanov has already pointed out this contradiction: *Neue Zeit* XVII, I, pp. 135ff). This contradiction is not immediately or directly overcome by the concrete expansion of our concrete knowledge. We saw that Kant likewise works with a correlate of in-itself and for-us – admittedly an undialectical, inflexible version – (whereby the participation of the in-itself in the emergence of and the objectivity of the for-us falls prey to a contradictory mythology) and he would without doubt perceive in Engels's alizarin nothing new in principle from the perspective of Newtonian astronomy, or his own astronomic theories. For from his perspective, the whole, infinitely expandable field of concrete knowledge is a world of objectivity, which merely, in relation to the thing-in-itself – which is at its basis and which stands *outside* knowledge, not taking into account concrete knowledge and its concrete expansion – remains tainted with the defect of subjectivity. Those who came after Kant and who wanted to make the thing-in-itself a mere limit concept of the theory of knowledge proceeded quite consistently in relation to the analysis of concrete knowledge. But they distorted Kant in as far as they simply screened out *his problem*, by not raising the question of the objective reality that is *independent of us*; and consequently they became dogmatic agnostics. It is thoroughly possible to be an agnostic in a philosophical sense in relation to reality, without bringing this agnosticism to bear on one's practical attitude to the external world, in particular scientific research and positions. Besides Engels explained this disparity clearly: 'No sooner – he says – is our agnostic done with his formal reservations, he speaks and acts as the hard-boiled materialist that he is at root' (*Neue Zeit* XI, I, p. 19).

Here Engels himself seems to admit that the agnostics merrily produce alizarin and yet – theoretically, philosophically – choose to remain agnostics. Therefore he has to be *philosophically* refuted. Engels points to Hegel's philosophical refutations of Kant's contradictions: 'if you know all the attributes of a thing then you know the thing itself; nothing else remains but the fact that said thing exists outside of us . . .' (ibid.). This philosophical refutation is a part of Hegel's dialectic of essence, his great outlining of the objectivity of appearance (cf. the relation of the thing-in-itself and essence, *Werke* II, Aufl. IV, p. 121). Of course, we cannot repeat Hegel's exposition here, not even in an abbreviated form. We have to limit ourselves to one essential point. This philosophical refutation and dissolution of the antinomies of the thing-in-itself pre-supposes that the subject–object relation is not metaphysically inflexible (as in Kant), but is understood as a dialectical interaction. The dialectical relativism of being and becoming, to which Hegel's argumentation amounts, presupposes the dialectical relativism of subject and substance (*Phenomenology of Spirit*). It is *on this* that the crux of Hegel's criticism of the thing-in-itself rests. Above all, Hegel counters the idea that the properties of a thing are purely subjective.

> A thing has *particularity*; *first of all* they are its specific relations to an *other*; the particularity is only present as a mode of behaviour towards an other; therefore it is an external reflection and part of the positedness of the thing. But *secondly*, the thing in its positedness is *in itself*; it contains itself in its relation to an other; but this is only a surface, with which existence is at the mercy of the becoming of being and change; the particularity does not thereby lose itself. A thing has the characteristic of effecting this or that in an other, and to externalise itself in a peculiar way in its relation. It evidences this particularity only under the condition of a corresponding composition of the other thing, but it is, at the same time, peculiar to it and its foundation which is identical to it, this reflected quality is therefore called a particularity. (*Phenomenology of Spirit*)

So Kant's problem is completely reversed, and precisely the thing-in-itself (in its Kantian version) appears as the subjective moment, as the product of abstract reflection; the thing-in-itself is 'as such nothing other than the empty abstraction of all determination, of which one can indeed know nothing, precisely because it is supposed to be the abstraction of all determination' (ibid.). This dialectical correlation is a moment of becoming. Only when becoming is understood as an over-reaching concrete moment can the inflexible opposition of object and subject be dialectically dissolved; that is why Hegel points out, in the passage first cited, that here 'existence is at the mercy of the becoming of being and change'. Neither Kant nor his contemporaries chose to recognise this. Plekhanov indicates correctly, however, that becoming is the point where the materialists of the eighteenth century 'were posed before the problem of the thing-in-itself and it was insoluble for them'. One can see this quite clearly in the passage cited above. Plekhanov shows, however, quite clearly that the limit of materialism's *theory of knowledge* is closely connected to the limit of its *conception of history* (the catastrophe theory of Holbach), the limit of their *conception of society* (dilemma of the relation between 'public opinion' – that is, a subjective factor – and social milieu – that is, an objective factor – ibid.). Hegel refutes Kant, not only by revealing the contradictions in his conception, but also by demonstrating – genetically – that this conception is a structure of knowledge that necessarily emerges from a particular stage of human understanding of the world. Only through this demonstration of the dialectic of the thing-in-itself – which remains unknown and unconscious for Kant – are those contradictions dissolved that for Kant had to appear as antinomies that are insoluble in principle. This genetic–dialectical refutation of Kant by Hegel remains, however, purely logical for Hegel. That means that he demonstrates that the Kantian conception of reality is one typical, possible and necessary position towards reality. However – despite numerous correct inklings – he provides no *concrete* genesis of this philosophy, no *historical* genesis. Only historical materialism's dialectic, placed on its feet, is in a position to do that. It alone is able to *concretise historically* what is correct in Hegel's exposition, and to prove that the conception of reality in Kant is not only a possible and typical position *vis-à-vis* objectivity, but is a concrete consequence of a concrete class position.

The agnostics are not refuted by experiment and industry but by clarification of the dialectic that lies in 'appearance'. And this clarification is itself a product of the revolutionising of social being, which owes its existence to experiment as much as industry, and which becomes conscious in the class consciousness of the proletariat – equally a product of this development – in the form of the for-itself. Therefore: it is not alizarin that is to be brought to consciousness about itself, as Comrade Rudas appears to think. Rather, as the proletariat reaches consciousness about itself, the in-itself–for-us relationship, mediated through those categories that expand the consciousness of the proletariat to a comprehensive dialectical consciousness of the totality of society in its relation to its natural foundation, secures its correct methodic position. It loses the agnostic character that it possessed in Kant as much as in the old materialists.

Experiment and industry are supposed to refute the philosophical crotchets of agnosticism by transforming in-itself to a for-us. Let us suppose that they do do this, then for whom do they do it? One would have to say quite logically: first of all for the experimenters themselves (I will not speak about industry for the time being). He who manufactures the alizarin must be immune to all the philosophical crotchets of agnosticism. But in reality this is not the case, as is well known. Since for Friedrich Engels the problem of the thing-in-itself is solved and dealt with by historical materialism, *for him* the experiment could *indeed* represent an example of the dialectical conception of reality. For the experimenter, however – if he does not happen to be a disciple of historical materialism – it does not go without saying. For the experiment in which the thing-in-itself becomes a thing-for-us is only in-itself dialectical. In order to reveal its *dialectical* character *for-us*, something else has to come along, something new – precisely historical materialism. Researchers into nature can carry out as many and as marvellous experiments as they like, and still, in spite of it all, cling on to the undiscernibility of the thing-in-itself, or be a Machist, or even Schopenhauerian. Lenin perceived this circumstance quite clearly: 'Not a *single word of any one* of these professors who are capable of carrying out the most valuable work in the specialist fields of chemistry, physics, history, *can be believed* as soon as it is a question of philosophy.' (CW 14, p. 342.) (I am quoting from Deborin's *Lenin: The Fighting Materialist*, because I cannot access Lenin's *Empiriocriticism* at the present moment.) Why? Because the experimenter is, namely, in a position to recognise objectively and correctly an objective partial cohesion in reality, but – as mere experimenter – is far from being in a position to say anything true and dialectical about the reality of that 'world of appearance' whose parts he researches correctly. This limitation, which lies in the nature of the pure experiment, I have characterised to the effect that it is not a praxis 'in a dialectical–philosophical sense', but rather a contemplative attitude and therefore, *as long as it remains merely contemplative*, is not able to overcome this limitation.

This entrapment in the limits of immediacy and its forms of thought is intensified if the experiment is used as a category of knowledge of society and history. This is understandable, for, on the one hand, the methodological precision that the experiment had in the natural sciences is lost (strict isolation of the objects under investigation, exclusion of interference, repetition under 'identical' conditions, etc.). On the other hand, the merely contemplative character comes more clearly to the fore, including the prevailing social attitude – which remains unconscious. It is well known that in the terminology of trade-union bureaucrats the Russian Revolution often figures as an 'experiment'. Given Deborin's preference for 'exact' terminology, it is surely axiomatic that he takes this over and uses it and virtually uses the lack of methodological preconditions for the experiment as his rationale. He says: 'Under certain conditions society can become the object of an experiment. Nature blocks our way as something alien. Experiments are only possible here within narrow limits. In social life relations are somewhat different. For there we people are ourselves primarily workers and creators. For history is made by humans, while nature is not made by them. Lenin is the great, ingenious experimenter. He submitted every theoretical case to a practical test' (*Lenin: The Fighting Materialist*). Here – under the disguise of enthusiasm for Lenin – creeps into our literature the ideology of the ossified trade-union bureaucrat, who does not dare openly to reject the Russian Revolution. For these have always – and from their perspective quite consistently – understood the Russian Revolution as an 'experiment'. Of course. For that releases them from any sort of activity. One just has to 'wait and see' if the experiment is successful. And if it 'fails' then things return to their previous state: one rabbit expired in spite of the inoculation with anti-toxin, but then if necessary one can find another rabbit, in order to 'observe' (but only observe) the effects of the social anti-toxin. The limitations of the contemplative attitude in modern science are what Marx specially emphasises in his critique of Feuerbach's contemplative materialism – but without inferring the brilliant [. . .] of method, for Deborin fetches his from bourgeois sociology. I cannot go into all moments of this critique here. I will merely cite the eighth thesis: 'All social life is essentially practical. All mysteries that lead theory to mysticism find their rational solution in human practice and in the comprehension of this practice.' With his usual comprehensive clarity, Marx stresses here that the comprehension of this praxis is correspondingly a precondition of the dissolution of those mysteries that exist everywhere for merely contemplative thought. (The passage is brilliantly illuminated by his criticism of the 'species concept' of Feuerbach 'as an internal *dumb* [my italics] generality which *naturally* unites the many individuals' (MECW 5, p. 5), and by the X and XI theses.)

From this state of affairs it does not follow that 'it is not the experiment that expands our knowledge, but rather *ideas* that direct us in the experiment', a position that Comrade Rudas ascribes to me (*Arbeiterliteratur* IX, p. 513). Nor does it mean that somehow, as a result of this extension beyond the limits of the mere experimenters, I now promote a 'proletarian physics', chemistry, etc. Lenin of all people points out splendidly in the passage cited above the difference between specialist sciences and philosophy. And here we are talking *only* about the *philosophical* question, given that Engels wants to use the experiment to refute precisely *philosophical* crotchets, and it is precisely the correctness of his philosophical refutation that I doubt. For it is clear (even Rudas admits it, *Arbeiterliteratur* IX, p. 511),[25] that Kant did not doubt the concrete expansion of our knowledge. We cannot envision that Kant would have disputed the expansion of knowledge through experiment by Newton's followers. (One might also think of Helmholtz who is on the whole a Kantian.) If then *despite this* Kant still denies the discernibility of the thing-in-itself, then he can *only* be refuted *philosophically* and not through mere experiment. His refutation begins, as we have shown, with Hegel, and is completed by Marx and Engels, who clarify *philosophically* what appearance is, what in-itself and for-us, etc., mean *concretely*, *in reality*, *historically*. (To what extent this refutation overcomes philosophy itself does not belong in our present discussion.)

The philosophical refutation of all philosophical crotchets transpires, as Marx shows in his Feuerbach critique, through revolutionary practice. Then the question arises: does the praxis of experiments (and of industry) mean a praxis *in this* sense, or – as I define it – in a dialectical–philosophical sense? Comrade Rudas thinks that he can discredit me with the question: 'Where is a praxis that is not subject to observation?' (*Arbeiterliteratur* IX, p. 512). Correct. But with this question, Rudas once more proves that he does not understand dialectics. As a faithful Kantian he contrasts the opposition of contemplative and practical behaviour along the lines of the dualistic schema of pure and practical reason. According to this conception, *everything* is revolutionising practice, even aborigines' kangaroo hunting, for in the night of Rudas's thought all cows are simply black. It is then quite incomprehensible why Marx emphasises a 'revolutionary practice' that has always existed, as something new, as an *opposition* to the way of seeing of the most developed society until now, bourgeois society (*Theses on Feuerbach*, Theses IX to X). Feuerbach really does base himself on a consistent materialism in his philosophy of nature. Why then does Marx point out, *versus* him, that he appeals to sensuous contemplation: 'but he does not conceive sensuousness as practical, human-sensuous activity' (Thesis V)? It is therefore a question of whether *this* praxis, which, according to the clear explanations of Marx, Feuerbach and the whole of contemplative materialism, *does not know*, is present in experiment (and industry), whether the 'lowest moonlighter', whom Comrade Rudas sets off against me with that noble indignation that we are now used to, who 'observes the effect of what he does' (*Arbeiterliteratur* IX, p. 512), adopts a practical attitude in *this* sense, in the sense of the Feuerbach Theses of Marx. Comrade Rudas is obviously of the opinion that if the activity of the moonlighter is 'practical', how much more so is that of the skilled labourer and the experimenter. It seems to me that Marx would hardly have grasped the 'observing' activity of the moonlighter as a revolutionary practice, as a practical–critical activity. For when he speaks in the passage quoted above of practice, he emphasises that the rational solution of mysteries finds itself 'in human practice and in the *comprehension* (my italics) of this practice'. And I hardly think that Marx would have understood the observing activity of the moonlighter as he breaks stones or some such thing as a comprehension of his praxis. Rather he would discern this comprehension only in knowledge of the social-historical process in its totality, in historical materialism. That is why Marx first sketches out (e.g. *Capital* I) how the capitalist division of labour automates the labour process, degrading the activity of the worker to supervision of the machine, and then he accents, in contrast to Dr Ure, the Pindar of the automated factory, how with the capitalist application of machinery on a large scale, and therefore with the modern factory system 'the automaton itself is the subject, and the workmen are merely conscious organs, coordinated with the unconscious organs of the automaton, and together with them, subordinated to the central moving power' (MECW 35, p. 422). It is simply farcical to believe that Marx would have imagined this activity (without comprehension of this praxis) to be revolutionary practice, to be an overcoming of Feuerbach.

Of course revolutionary practice grows on the basis of a social being that motivates this activity. But not elementally, not spontaneously, rather precisely through the workers becoming conscious of the social, historical preconditions of their activity, the objective tendencies of economic development, which have motivated their activity and which push beyond these forms of social being, become *conscious*, and *extend* this consciousness (comprehension of praxis: class consciousness) to revolutionary practice. The experimenter lacks this consciousness of the basis of his activity; that is to say he has it if he is 'coincidentally' a Marxist (coincidentally because his class situation does not contain any objective social necessity). He observes a part of objective reality, and in as far as he has correctly observed it, he reaches correct scientific results, just as the worker, if he correctly serves the automaton, whose little part he has become, helps to complete the prescribed task of work correctly. The material substructure of both processes is dialectical: it is a moment in an objective dialectical process. The dialectic of the capitalist process of labour, of capitalist technology, etc., has even become – in historical materialism – a dialectical knowledge. But both processes are dialectical only in-themselves. And this being-in-itself is in no way overcome by adopting an immediate-conscious form. The experimenter transforms his partial aspect of the in-itself to a for-us, without the dialectical character of the whole context – to which belong the object of his activity, his activity and the categories in which he becomes conscious of it – having become dialectically conscious. Even when the whole in its connections is present, the immediate form of its becoming conscious need not coincide with its actual inner structure. For example, in a letter to Lassalle, Marx speaks of the system that Heraclitus and Epicurus had 'only in-itself' and stresses that even with philosophers like Spinoza, whose thought has a systematic form, the 'actual inner structure of his system [is] quite different to the form in which it was consciously presented by him' (Gustav Mayer's *Nachlaß-Ausgabe* III). The dialectical transformation of the in-itself into a for-us always requires more than an immediate transposition into forms of consciousness.

The mere researcher into nature lacks consciousness about the material foundations of his activities. And his activity alone cannot give him this consciousness, still less than the worker can arrive at class consciousness through the mere labour process and the spontaneous elemental struggles against the employers, although both – objectively – are moments of the dialectical process whose product is class consciousness. Of course: still less can there be any sort of philosophy or epistemology that can very often mislead researchers, who have achieved much of value in their specialist area, to the most brazen and most absurd conclusions. Consciousness *can only* be provided by historical materialism. For the researcher of nature is just as much a product of his social being as any normal mortal. I do not want to talk at all about the personal, class-derived prejudices that influence his thought, especially when he leaves his specialist area and begins to philosophise. But these rarely hinder him in generating *objectively correct* knowledge in his specialist area, in transforming an in-itself into a for-us. I mean much more that his consciousness too is determined by his social being; that, though he is of the opinion that he confronts objective reality, nature, without predispositions, impartially, he remains caught up, to the greatest possible extent, in the immediately given forms of his social being – which are invisible to him – just as was the case for the most shining representatives of classical economy in England in their day. That *specialist research* in the natural sciences, leading to impartial and therefore objective, correct results, is still possible, has its basis in the metabolic relationship between society and nature, which tends in our transitional period to the process of revolutionising society, that I indicated above. Only historical materialism, in which the social knowledge of the proletariat as knowledge for-itself comes to expression, is able to create clarity here. Only historical materialism cares to work out the real origin and therefore the concrete essence of the categories of our being and our consciousness. Forms of thought, accepted in their immediacy as natural, as eternal, are elucidated as products of the social-historical process of development. Just how deeply the historically changing, therefore historically ephemeral process of *capitalist* exchange of matter with nature determines our present knowledge of nature, and where those categories that determine the metabolic exchange *of any society* with nature begin, are questions for individual research. This will probably show that some categories that appear today as 'eternal', as categories directly taken from nature, e.g. work in physics, are actually historical, determined by the specific exchange of matter between capitalist society and nature. Marx detected in Descartes's conception of animals a reflection of the period of manufacture (*Capital* I), and he regards Lamettrie's conception of humans as a direct continuation of this Cartesian tradition (*The Holy Family*). Kautsky too, when he was still a Marxist, thought 'that as long as the bourgeoisie was revolutionary theories of catastrophe dominate in the natural sciences; and they were dissolved by the theories of imperceptible development, once the bourgeoisie were diverted into conservative tracks. This connection will surprise no one who knows how much social needs and feelings influence not only social but also natural scientific theories, the whole world picture' (*Neue Zeit* XXIII, II, p. 134).

Only through such a knowledge of the material foundations of the natural sciences and, with them, the foundations of the experiment, which – I repeat – *only* historical materialism is in a position to afford, does the dialectical context which underpins a single result or a whole area in itself, become a *dialectical* context for us too. However, in addition, the 'higher' category of for-itself is a precondition for the class consciousness of the proletariat that cannot be waived. Such a transformation, though, of the in-itself into a for-us, carried out by experiment and industry, *comprises* the material, the matter of practical overcoming of the philosophical crotchets, as Marx always indicates genetically, in his dialectical dissolution of bourgeois economy, in pointing out the dialectic, which was contained in it in-itself, but only in-itself. And he always treats correct and false theories in connection with their material underpinning, showing why social being makes it possible for one person to discover the correct connection correctly, and why another person must be hindered, either in understanding the contradiction at all, or in becoming conscious of its dialectical character.

These arguments spare us an extensive investigation of industry as revolutionary practice. Comrade Rudas reproaches me with a *quid pro quo* because in my polemic against Engels's passage I equate industry with capitalist. (I admit that 'capitalist industry' would have been a more accurate expression.) He maintains: in any case it is completely irrelevant whether industry is capitalist or not, saying that 'A communist industry will act just as does a capitalist one or whatever type – in the sense of industry that Engels uses here . . . . For in this sense, industry is an eternal nature-imposed necessity, without which there can be no material exchanges between man and nature' (*Arbeiterliteratur* IX, pp. 514–15). In the first place, the reference to Marx is incorrect. Marx says: 'The fact that the production of *use values*, or goods, is carried on under the control of a capitalist and on his behalf, does not alter the *general character* of that production. We shall, therefore, in the first place have to *consider* the labour process independently of the particular form it assumes under given social conditions' (*Capital* I, MECW 35, p. 187; italics are mine). For Marx it is a case of a 'sensible abstraction' with which, for reasons of method, he can begin his investigation and then later develop all the specific determinations that concretely reproduce historical actuality. It is impossible to relate Engels's passage to this type of methodical abstraction. If the praxis of industry is supposed to refute philosophical crotchets, then that can be done only by *actual* industry and not by the abstract concept of a production of use values. And I do not agree that it would be a misunderstanding to equate actual industry and the capitalist industry in this concrete relation.

Every time that Marx speaks *concretely* about industry, he speaks clearly and unambiguously about capitalist industry. I will leave to one side the fundamental passages about the division of labour and will point only briefly to his treatment of machinery, for there it appears most tempting to suppose that it is a case of a – if not superhistorical form – then at least a form of being that functions identically in capitalism and socialism; socialism will naturally also have to work with machines. I will cite only a few important passages:

> The lightening of the labour, even, becomes a form of torture, since the machine does not free the labourer from work, but deprives the work of all interest. Every kind of capitalist production in so far as it is not only a labour process, but also a process of creating surplus value, has this in common, that it is not the workman that employs the instruments of labour, but the instruments of labour that employ the workman. But it is only in the factory system that this inversion for the first time acquires technical and palpable reality. By means of its conversion into an automaton, the instrument of labour confronts the labourer, during the labour process, in the shape of capital, of dead labour, that dominates, and pumps dry, living labour power. The separation of the intellectual powers of production from the manual labour, and the conversion of those powers into the might of capital over labour, is, as we have already shown, finally completed by modern industry erected on the foundation of machinery. (*Capital* I, MECW 35, p. 426)

And:

> And this is the point relied on by our apologists! The contradictions and antagonisms inseparable from the capitalist employment of machinery, do not exist, they say, since they do not arise out of machinery, as such, but out of its capitalist employment! Since therefore machinery, considered alone, shortens the hours of labour, but, when in the service of capital, lengthens them; since in itself it lightens labour but when employed by capital, heightens the intensity of labour; since in itself it is a victory of man over the forces of nature, but in the hands of capital, makes man the slave of those forces; since in itself it increases the wealth of the producers, but in the hands of capital, makes them paupers – for all these reasons and others besides, says the bourgeois economist without more ado, it is clear as noonday that all these contradictions are a mere semblance of the reality, and

that, as a matter of fact, they have neither an actual nor a theoretical existence. (MECW 35, p. 444)

These passages show that Marx always scrupulously bore in mind the 'capitalist husk' of the productive forces, when studying its concrete form. It is clear that this capitalist husk is merely a husk, that 'behind' this husk (better inside this husk) those objective social forces that brought about capitalism, and which will lead to its demise, are effective. But it confuses those who conclude from this fact the 'subjective', illusory character of this husk; as do the Kantians, like Comrade Rudas. The materialist dialectician knows that the capitalist husk is just as much a part of objective reality (just as with Hegel the appearance is a moment of the essence), but only dialectically correct knowledge of the whole in all its concrete determinations is in a position to grasp mentally the type and degree, etc., of objectivity and of the actuality of the individual moments. Through such correct dialectical knowledge of the capitalist husk it is recognised in its actuality as husk. That is to say, it becomes clear that knowledge of its social determinedness does not turn it into a mere illusion (something subjective), that knowledge of its transitoriness does not change the fact that it *is a concrete form of industry for our epoch*, and that actual industry can *only* be separated from this husk *conceptually*. For the existence of this husk is inseparably tied up with the most essential forms of existence of our present social being. (Machines with division of labour in factories, division of labour in factories with social division of labour, etc.) With historical materialism we can reach an outlook on to those times where these real forms of being are really abolished (higher phase of communist society in the *Critique of the Gotha Programme*), but we cannot pre-empt this development concretely in thought. The actual disappearance of the capitalist husk happens in the *real process of history*: that is to say, in order to allow the capitalist husk to disappear concretely and actually those real categories of social being (capitalist division of labour, separation of town and country, of physical and mental labour) must be revolutionised. This revolutionising must, of course, also revolutionise to a large extent (technically as well) the concrete form of industry (relationship of technology to capitalist division of labour). For both epochs, only the *concept* of agricultural industry, industry as a 'sensible abstraction' remains the same.

Comrade Rudas's objection, his ignorance of the dialectic of the capitalist husk, reveals clearly his 'unconscious intention', the – illogical, unscientific – basis of his misunderstanding: *his* tail-ending *turns into apologia*. In treating the capitalist husk as a mere appearance, which one simply needs to strip away like a veil, in order to perceive *concretely* 'industry' as an 'objective process of production', 'eternal nature-imposed exchanges between man and nature', Comrade Rudas's efforts lead to spelling out the *essential identity of capitalist society and communist society*. He reveals that its *concrete* shape is the *same* in capitalism and socialism. He imagines that he has achieved a special materialist insight into the social process of development, when he merely leaves out of the picture – as do all apologists – the specific historical determinations of capitalism. It is the same mistake – theoretically – as that of the opportunistic trade-union bureaucrats, who in 1918 professed to find themselves in the 'middle of socialism'. Obviously for Rudas, as for Deborin, activity, praxis is no more than the 'struggle of society with nature' (*Arbeiterliteratur* X, p. 639). He *can* and simply *will* not imagine another form of the process of social development than the fatalistic elementary process of capitalism. He does not want to leave his noble scientific post as 'observer' of the law-bound course of history, whereby he can 'anticipate' revolutionary developments. Actual transformation, inasmuch as it exists for him, is provided for already by the development of the base. Everything that disturbs this tailist peace is idealism, agnosticism, dualism, etc.

In my remarks on the passage from Engels (using a quotation from Engels himself) I pointed to precisely this *elemental* character of *capitalist* industry. Self-evidently in so doing I did not commit the stupidity that Comrade Rudas, for reasons that are now understandable, ascribes to me. I did not deny the expansion of our knowledge by capitalist industry. I must, however, return to what I said earlier about experiments; does this expansion of our knowledge denote a philosophical refutation of the philosophical crotchets of Kant and other thinkers? I will repeat here too: yes, for he who stands on the ground of historical materialism, he who – unlike Comrade Rudas who confuses the abstract concept of

industry with its real-historical form – conceives the development of
capitalist industry in its dialectical antagonisms. For the question that
was thrown up earlier is valid to an even greater degree here: why does
the development of industry not refute the philosophical crotchets, first
and foremost, for those who 'carry out' industry; why do these people –
and not only the owners of capital but also the actual leaders of industry, captains of industry, engineers, etc., fall victim to the philosophical
crotchets of agnosticism to an increasing degree as capitalism develops?
We can only repeat our earlier answer: because to an increasing degree
it becomes impossible for them to become conscious of the real, material
foundations of their existence objectively, in class terms; because agnosticism with all its philosophical crotchets is the necessary form of their
class compromise with their feudal forebears, because they are the bear-
ers of this development – 'with no will of their own and without
resistance' – they are objects of the real dialectic that rules here and not
its subjects. Moreover their praxis appears inseparable from its capitalist husk.

All this, one might with justification counter, was better known by
Friedrich Engels than the author of these modest remarks. That is correct. But precisely because of that, in the passage of my book that has
been mentioned, it was I who introduced Engels's early work in order to
counter the theory analysed here. For it seems to me that Engels, as he
tested the dialectical method out on knowledge of nature in a ripe old
age, sometimes took the route that led him to his command of the
dialectic too much for granted to work things out specifically in his
depictions. He says, for example, about the dialectic:

> It is, however, precisely the polar antagonisms put forward as irrecon-
> cilable and insoluble, the forcibly fixed lines of demarcation and class
> distinctions, that have given modern theoretical natural science its
> restricted, metaphysical character. The recognition that these antago-
> nisms and distinctions, though to be found in nature, are only of relative
> validity, and that *on the other hand their imagined rigidity and absolute validity*
> *have been introduced into nature only by our reflective minds* – this recognition is
> the kernel of the dialectical conception of nature. (*Anti-Dühring*, MECW
> 25, p. 14 – my italics)

Now this state of affairs, whose social character, as one can see, is quite clearly emphasised by Engels, lies at the basis of precisely the decisive parts of the dialectical logic of Hegel, the logic of essence, which Engels – in the letter to Lange quoted above – characterises as Hegel's 'philosophy of nature'. It is, though, not only his true philosophy of nature, but also his actual philosophy of society. It is no accident that the highpoint of knowledge in bourgeois society, the 'objective spirit', adopts a middle position between nature and 'absolute spirit' in the system, just as the logic of essence adopts the middle position between the logic of being and the logic of the concept. Precisely because – unbeknownst to Hegel of course – here the real laws of movement, the real social being of bourgeois society mirror themselves conceptually in the 'logic of essence'. If Marx, in overturning Hegel's philosophy, has at the same time rescued its real core, then he precisely rescued most from the logic of essence – demythologised, of course. For here in purely mental, in mythological–mystified form is precisely a reflection of the social being of bourgeois society. (I hope to be able to outline one day thoroughly the relationship of Marx to Hegelian logic.)

For Engels then, this partial omission of the mediations that made his dialectical knowledge possible, that objectively belong to this knowledge, is just one episode. And if only Engels were involved, then one could quite calmly lay this question to rest, or let it remain an inessential historical, philological question. Since, however, these flaws enthusiastically multiply, and are raised up into the system of Marxism, *for the purposes of liquidating the dialectic*, these points had to be clearly chronicled. For the tendency of Deborin and Rudas is clear: using the *words* of Marx and Engels, they want to turn historical materialism into a 'science' in the bourgeois sense, because they cannot relinquish the basics of life in bourgeois society and its conception of history. They cannot relinquish the purely elemental character of historical happening, because they – [. . .]

[Ms breaks off]

Notes

1. Rudas writes:

In Germany's philosophical world Comrade Lukács enjoyed a well-earned name as a philosopher, long before he was a communist, and indeed he is known as a philosopher who followed his own path, who thinks independently, and does not simply chew over what great thinkers have bequeathed to posterity. Then, Comrade L. became a communist. As such he worked illegally for our party already before the Hungarian proletarian revolution. In and after the Hungarian revolution he always occupied an exposed position. He never wavered for a minute. He was always an avowed enemy of opportunism. If his philosophical past awakens a quiet mistrust of his philosophical future, it must be noted that he did fight as a communist for the proletarian revolution in dangerous posts, as both people's commissar and as soldier at the front, and he proved himself in other ways too.

2. Rudas writes: 'A word on the "misunderstandings" – they are not at all, as people commonly erroneously think, of a logical type. No – Bernstein was "misunderstood" by Kautsky, Kautsky, for his part, by Lenin ("The Renegade Kautsky etc.") and Trotsky ("Anti-Kautsky"). In fact, the misunderstanding arose from the fact that Lenin showed that Kautsky is *objectively* a renegade. But Kautsky is *subjectively* still of the opinion today that he is not one. That is indeed a small misunderstanding.'

3. Deborin writes:

As genuine 'orthodox thinkers', in contrast to this Engels fellow, they reproach 'naïve' materialism, defending instead the identity of subject and object, of thought and being. Hereby, as we have already seen, they call on Marx, whose teachings were perverted or misunderstood by Engels. We have already satisfied ourselves as to how far this is fitting. The wholly unfounded counterpoising of Engels and Marx must be decisively refuted. Marx never argued for the identity of subject and object, of thought and being. That is pure *idealism*, which may be proclaimed by devout Hegelians after the fashion of Lukács and his followers, but which was completely alien to Marx. Lenin quite correctly protested against just such a position as represented in A. Bogdanov, with whom Lukács has a great deal in common. On the identity of being and knowledge, Lenin writes: ' "Social being" and "social consciousness" are not identical, just as being in general and consciousness in general are not identical. From the fact that in their intercourse men act as conscious beings, it *does not follow* that social consciousness is identical with social being. In all social formations of any complexity – and in the capitalist social formation in particular – people in their intercourse are *not conscious* of what kind of social relations are being formed, in accordance with what laws they develop, etc. . . . Social consciousness *reflects* social being – that is Marx's teaching.

A reflection may be an approximately true copy of the reflected, but to speak of identity is absurd. Consciousness in general *reflects* being – that is a general principle of *all* materialism.' (From Lenin's *Materialism and Empirio-Criticism*.)

4. Lukács now italicises the words 'at all' in this citation from HCC. Rodney Livingstone does not translate the original 'überhaupt' in this passage, so here the quotation has been modified. [Trans.]

5. Rudas writes:

> Indeed, even the transition from the realm of necessity to the 'realm of freedom', so beloved of him and so important to him, is imagined as a 'moment'. ('When the moment of transition to the "realm of freedom" arrives . . .' HCC p. 70). But one would be pretty despairing of the 'fate of the revolution, indeed of humanity' – if it really depends on moments. For some moments may be correctly apprehended, but most of them will certainly be missed! We no longer have a Lenin at our disposal who would be in a position to correctly assess the moments. What is to be done? The revolution is doomed to defeat and along with that humanity is probably condemned to ruination. What a tragic prospect! This irrevocable theory of the moment has a desperate similarity to the theory of great personalities, on the one hand, and on the other hand to Max Weber's various non-repeating constellations. The entire bourgeoisie hoped that with the death of Lenin the proud edifice of the Russian Revolution would collapse. But no, it stands stronger than ever. The bourgeoisie made a mistake because the role of even the most epochal personalities is not that ascribed to them by the bourgeoisie. But the role of the 'moment' cannot be a different one or a greater one than that of the greatest personalities. In an entire epoch of social revolution, where the powerfully developed productive forces of modern economy push for a resolution – and do so ever more strongly – even the most important 'moments' cannot contain enough to 'crucially decide' the outcome of class struggle. (Rudas, *Arbeiterliteratur* XII, pp. 1077–8)

6. The word Lukács uses for 'moment' in this context is 'Augenblick'. On other occasions, he uses the philosophical term 'Moment'. It has been impossible always to preserve this distinction in the present text, as the edition of HCC quoted in the text does not allow observation of the difference between 'Augenblick' and 'Moment'. [Trans.]

7. Rudas quotes Lenin against Lukács: 'The economic foundation of this use of revolutionary force, the guarantee of its effectiveness and success is the fact that the proletariat represents and creates a higher type of social organisation of labour compared with capitalism. *This is what is important, this is the source of the strength and the guarantee that the final triumph of communism is inevitable.*' ('A Great Beginning', 1919.) Rudas adds: 'And not in consciousness or "only" with conscious will!' He then continues with the quote from Lenin.

Clearly, in order to abolish classes completely, it is not enough to overthrow the exploiters, the landowners and capitalists, not enough to abolish *their* rights of ownership; it is necessary also to abolish all private ownership of the means of production, it is necessary to abolish the distinction between town and country, as well as the distinction between manual workers and brain workers. *This requires a very long period of time. In order to achieve this an enormous step forward must be taken in developing the productive forces* . . . for this ability does not come of itself, but grows historically, and grows *only* out of the material conditions of large-scale capitalist production. This ability, at the beginning of the road from capitalism to socialism, is possessed by the proletariat *alone*. (Ibid.)

8. For example, Rudas writes:

As is evident in the name, something that is unknown is 'imputed' from something else that is known. The name stems from mathematics, where it means the easiest thing in the world. Suppose that two rows of numbers x and y have a particular relationship to one another such that to each value of x corresponds a value of y. This is known to be the case when x and y stand in a functional relationship to one another, such that, we say

$$F(x) = y.$$

If I know various values of x, whereby x takes on the values 1, 2, 3 in succession, then the values of y are *imputed* to those values of x. This is not always an easy mathematical task. Whether it is difficult or easy is not an issue for us here, since we aim only to clarify the concept. In every problem of imputation therefore there must be something (x) that is known and something (y) that is unknown and which must be 'imputed' from the former. Right now I need to emphasise something else, which will be of importance to us in what follows, for it is an *essential* feature of this problem and we will have much cause to stress precisely this feature: both *amounts x and y stand, of course, in mathematics not in a causal relationship, but in a functional relationship to each other.* A causal relationship would not make sense in mathematics. Irrespective of what the cause of the transformation of x may be, this transformation pulls the transformation of y along with it without one having to say that the *cause* of the transformation of y is x. To each value of x a value of y *corresponds* – but not every transformation of x *causes* the transformation of y. In mathematics, where nothing happens, this is quite befitting. But now the philosopher and the sociologist, Rickert and Weber, have not only appropriated this concept of 'imputation' from mathematics into philosophy and sociology, but they have taken it over with all its mathematical logic and precisely with the intention either to totally eradicate or at least demote to a second (insignificant) rung *causality* from the world of social appearances! In history too (at best) the causal relation is turned into a functional relation. The 'problem of imputation' is used by them to deny the exact causal obedience to law precisely of social occurrences, to make history a philosophy of history, i.e. a *metaphysics* of history. And sociology is demoted from a science which contains the general laws of social occurrence to a 'science' which denies any lawful knowledge of social occurrence. And, as if given by god, they receive the mathematical concept of 'imputation' and precisely the characteristic of this concept, which in mathematics is its highly logical conse-quence – the characteristic namely that known and unknown, which are imputed from each other, stand in no causal connection with each other! For they who deny social appearance's obedience to laws, indeed, precisely the *concept of causality* is a thorn in the eye! (Rudas, *Arbeiterliteratur* X, pp. 670–71)

9. Rudas writes:

Just as in the natural sciences, so in the Marxist science of society, causality (or mutual interaction) is a natural or social force that is effective in reality. It brings phe-nomena into certain relationships with each other, and this relationship is *given* in reality, is *not alterable*, and our task can only consist in seeking out this relation-ship *empirically*, and not to *construct* it according to an 'aim of knowledge'. This relationship is a general one, i.e. it is not only a singular fact, but rather whole rows of facts are in causal dependence on each other. Such relationships can therefore be expressed through a *general law*. Such a law is, for example, Darwin's law of devel-opment or the Marxist law of the dependency between the process of production and the political, or where relevant, spiritual process of the social realm. Therefore, neither in the natural sciences nor in Marxism does the problem of 'imputation' appear as it does in the Rickertians and in Weber. *What* is cause and *what* is effect in a complex of social events is never questionable in Marxism; nor is what is significant and what insignificant in this complex. Mind you, a question can perhaps arise about whether a concrete fact is to be derived from this or that cause. *However, the law-bound sequence of the connection of the complex of events is not in doubt.* Neither that they stand in a causal connection, nor *how*, nor in what sequence they are connected. This sequence is clearly fixed in Marx's social doctrine. And this doctrine is an empirical theory, devised from experience, which wishes only to express what is, and what is really embodied in the phenomena. In this respect Marxism is pure natural science.

10. Rudas writes:

A sheep and a person – they are both components of nature. Or, as the French poet, Francis Jammes, in whom lives a materialist soul, has expressed it: 'Oh, you poor donkeys, you are all my brothers!' And if natural laws have so worked dialec-tically with sheep that they have 'instinct', then it is the case with humans that their 'instinct' has become a 'consciousness'. What Marx and Engels always want to stress is clear: nature and society (sheep and person) are not only not different from each other, but they are *fundamentally the same*. They say it quite concisely . . .

11. See note 9.

12. The German translation of Lenin speaks of 'dreamy sentimentality' where the English translation uses 'Manilovism'. Manilovism is from the name of the land-lord Manilov in Gogol's *Dead Souls*, who was the embodiment of philistinism, smug complacency and futile daydreaming. [Trans.]

13. Rudas writes:

What is a 'historical role'? A role that like every other one, takes place independently of – although also through – human consciousness of this role. What can it mean to speak of the 'sense' of this role? It means two things. The *materialists* say: the same thing, which is objective, that is to say independent from, how people understand it, occurs, is simultaneously grasped by people who have the capacity to think. If stones fall on an inclined plane – then the laws of gravity are known. If thrones and human heads fall – then the social laws, the laws of revolution, are known. This 'knowing' is its 'sense' – nothing else. And this sense is – as already said – a psychic process in people, whose capacity for thought is stirred by events. But just as this psy-chic process is itself only another (particularly qualified) side of the physiological process, and not something *above* this physiological process, something *supersensuous*, so too a knowledgeable, purposive process is nothing other than the *objective process itself, as it is known by people*. Therefore the materialists say: 'The historical role' of a class and the 'sense' of this historical role are *not* different from one another. But the idealists say: They *are different* from one another. Every 'process' must have a 'sense', that is, *strive towards a goal*. It is not possible that the world (nature and society) should have no end goal towards which it strives; no purpose: that would be 'senseless'. If we investigate a natural or historical process, then something else exists outside the causal connection of events and above it: the goal towards which the event in ques-tion strives. The purpose that nature and society possess, and which the event in question helps to accomplish. And only those events that help to accomplish this aim or purpose are 'significant' or 'historically significant'. As we see, these are the so-called 'values', 'cultural values' etc. that we got to know in Rickert and Weber. But when Comrade L. says: 'class consciousness is the sense, become conscious, of the historical role of the class', then he says – according to the citation above – either this, that the 'sense of the historical role' is such value judgements, or, simply, he is referring to knowledge of the unfolding of social events and their tendencies in obe-dience to the law. Even in this case class consciousness is something more. We will have more to say about this. By and large I would be in agreement with him, of course. But, then, what is so astounding is that this simple fact is formulated in such an idealistic and misleading way. Precisely in order to avoid this evil-smelling danger, Marxists would favour another language. That would say: each stage of the pro-ductive forces that is achieved pushes society in a certain direction (perceivable by theory). This direction is 'higher' or 'lower', 'progression' or 'regression', according to circumstances. That is its 'sense' – nothing else. This direction (= tendency) is knowable, it can be made conscious. . . . But I ask: '*where is* it become conscious? *In whom is* it become conscious? *How* has it become conscious?'

Either it has become conscious in single individuals (let us say proletarians) or it has become conscious in the whole class. Is there a third possibility? Until now people were not conscious of their historical role. Why not, and what they were conscious of instead is quite another question. Now they become aware of it for some reason or another. Does that not amount to saying that now can be found in their heads different, *real-psychological* thoughts, feelings, aims, etc., which correspond better or more perfectly to reality than those of days gone by? Can the words 'become conscious' mean something else too? That these new thoughts, feelings, aims, etc., can be *summed up* in the phrase 'sense of the historical role' changes nothing about the fact that it will be and must be consciously experienced, that is to say, *psychologically*, if it has become conscious. If that is, however, the case, then Comrade L. commits once more – as so often – one of his usual logical (side)steps. Just for a change, this step is not called equivocation or *quid pro quo*, but quite simply – *contradiction*. And, to be sure, it is not a dialecticai contradiction. Comrade L. denies in the first part of his sentence what he acknowledges in the second part. The first part of the sentence *completely* contradicts the second part. In the first part it is claimed that class consciousness is neither the psychological consciousness of individual people nor the mass-psychological one of many people. Now one might believe that Comrade L. has discovered a third place, where class consciousness realises itself. Perhaps in the head of a God or many gods, perhaps in the head of Madame History, or some such thing. No. In the second part of his sentence he admits what has been denied in the first part. For it says: class consciousness is 'the sense, become conscious, of the historical role of the class'. It can, however – as said – be the head of the person (whether as an individual psychology or mass-psychologically) only where class consciousness is realised, where something becomes conscious for them. Only that which becomes conscious for them, that is to say, only the content of consciousness is further defined by L. in the second part of the passage: that is, the 'sense of the historical role of the class'. But that, if you please, is a different situation! What the content of consciousness of the person is at any one moment, whether this content corresponds to reality or not, that is a question in itself, which has absolutely nothing at all to do with the question of whether consciousness is psychological or mass-psychological! The content may be true or false, it may express a 'sense of the historical role of the class' or not, but the consciousness that accommodates this content is either an individual psychological or mass-psychological one! There is only one case where it is not so: if the 'sense of the historical role of the class' 'becomes conscious' such that it itself, this sense, becomes a separate, special consciousness, different from the individual consciousness of the person and enthroned above the heads of people. Then we have a (hidden) god before us! (Philosophically that is called hypostatising.) In the best (or worst) scenario the 'imputed' consciousness of Comrade L. is a hypostatised consciousness – which is,very similar to a divine consciousness. (Rudas, *Arbeiterliteratur* X, extracts from pp. 678–82)

14. Rudas writes:

Let us listen to how Lenin characterises the situation and the consciousness of the peasants. We will see immediately where the difference lies between a Marxist materialist and a philosophical Idealist:
'The situation of the peasants is constituted according to their being, their conditions of production, their life conditions, the conditions of their economy, such that the peasant is a half-worker, half-speculator.'
'*The peasants – are a particular class.* As workers they are enemies of capitalist exploitation, but at the same time they are themselves property-owners. The peasant has been brought up for hundreds of years in the belief that the bread belongs to him and that he is at liberty to sell it. That is my right – the peasant thinks, for that is my labour, my sweat and blood. *To quickly overcome his psychology is impossible*, that is a long and difficult struggle.'
'The question is such that the peasant is used to free trade in bread.'
'The peasant is half-worker, half-speculator. The peasant is a worker because he attains his bread through sweat and blood; he is exploited by the landowners, capitalists and traders. The peasant is – a speculator because he sells the bread, this use object . . .'
(Lenin, 'On Deceiving the People with the Slogans of Liberty and Equality')
Firstly: here the peasantry is recognised to be a 'particular class'. According to L., it is however questionable whether 'it can be considered a class at all in the strict Marxist sense'. But I note that only in passing.
Secondly: what does the particular class psychology signify here ('To quickly overcome his psychology is impossible'), other than the class consciousness of the peasants? (Rudas, *Arbeiterliteratur* X, p. 691)

15. For example, Rudas complains:

Adler, as a Kantian, perceives in consciousness something that is prior to any socialisation and that even before socialisation already possesses the character of – being socialised! As is known the consciousness of humans arose long *after* their socialisation, long after humans had not only lived communally, but also worked communally. It arose after or at least at the same time as language. This, for its part, arose slowly, through a painstaking development lasting thousands of years. It emerged from animal sounds, which slipped out of people as they expended purely mechanical, biological effort while they worked, and these sounds were fixed for the purpose of understanding during the communal labour process and thus became 'words'. This is what Marx and Engels say:
'From the start the "spirit" is afflicted with the curse of being "burdened" with matter, which here makes its appearance in the form of agitated layers of air, sounds, in short, of language. Language is as old as consciousness, language is practical consciousness that exists also for other men, and for that reason alone it

really exists for me personally as well; language, like consciousness, only arises from the need, the necessity, of intercourse with other men. (*German Ideology*)

That is the language of materialists. (Rudas, *Arbeiterliteratur* XII, p. 1070)

16. This is a reference to the leader of the Bulgarian Peasant Party, Alexandur Stambulisky. Stambulisky, Prime Minister of Bulgaria between 1919 and 1923, attempted to create a 'dictatorship of the peasantry'. He was murdered in June 1923. [Trans.]

17. Translation slightly altered from Rodney Livingstone's version in order to fit in with what follows. [Trans.]

18. Rudas quotes Lukács:

'For only "when consciousness stands in such a relation to reality can theory and praxis be united". For this to happen the emergence of consciousness must become the decisive step which the historical process must take towards its proper end (an end constituted by the wills of men, but neither dependent on human whim, nor the product of human invention). The historical function of theory is to make this step a practical possibility. Only when a historical situation has arisen in which a class must understand society if it is to assert itself; only when the fact that a class understands itself means that it understands society as a whole and when, in consequence, the class becomes both the subject and object of knowledge; in short, only when these conditions are all satisfied will the unity of theory and praxis, the precondition of the revolutionary function of the theory, become possible.' [HCC, pp. 2–3]

One must excuse me this long quote. It had to be cited, for here Comrade L. displays himself, not only in his covert conclusions, but also quite openly as an idealist, an idealist, to whom 'theory' represents what for the idealists of the old stripe was the idea. For firstly his starting point, for all that he says about the historical process, is always and consistently theory and never praxis. The practical essence of theory must be extracted from theory and not from praxis. (Just let me mention in passing: that is a contradiction in terms, if the practical essence of theory must be extracted out of theory and not developed through theory.) Its relationship to objects and not the reverse is the decisive thing. (In the second extract we will see that Comrade L. denies praxis altogether, when, according to the pattern of all genuine idealists, he simply dissolves it into theory, or even into thought.) Theory is the motivating force behind the masses and there is 'no necessary connection' with other factors. If the masses are 'in the grip of quite different forces' than those of theory 'they act towards different goals' than those of theory, that is to say: if they are motivated by social laws, which are 'necessary or fortuitous' – then theory is not 'genuinely and necessarily' bound to the masses. Secondly, though, consciousness is the decisive step, which the historical process makes towards its proper end; the historical function of theory consists in making the step of history towards its proper end a 'practical possibility' etc. etc. (Rudas, *Arbeiterliteratur* IX, pp. 505–6)

19. Lukács is not quoting from the original *German Ideology* but from an excerpt in Gustav Mayer's *Engels*, vol. 1. The quotation is a collage of sentences from pages 62–4. [Trans.]

20. Rudas writes: 'If the dialectic is restricted to society, then two worlds exist, with two quite different sets of laws: nature and society. In nature phenomena are undialectical, in society they are dialectical. Fine. All the great philosophers may have been monists, but that does not mean that they were right. According to L. the world is dualist.'

21. Rudas writes:

L. says quite explicitly that the cause of the dialectic's arrival is the human being. [. . .] he enumerates the following 'crucial determinants' of dialectics:

1. Interaction of subject and object. (He accuses even Engels of neglecting this interaction.)
2. Unity of theory and praxis.
3. Historical changes in the reality underlying the categories as the root cause of changes in thought. (What this philosophical thieves' Latin means is utterly irrelevant for us here, for it suffices to decipher that 'a change in thought is the matter under discussion'. Only people can think, and that suffices completely for our purposes.)
4. 'Etc.' This 'etc.' is unfortunately very inappropriate, for perhaps here we might have the 'crucial' characteristics of the dialectic that do not depend on humans.

The characteristics listed as 1–3 obviously only relate to humans. Only humans have praxis and theory, only humans can speak of subject and object, thought exists only for humans. But I have no idea why for all the world precisely these three are the 'crucial determinants of dialectics', as Comrade L. maintains, and not the 'fluidity' of the concept, the negation of the negation, the transformation of quantity into quality, etc. I will not even dare to express my suspicions. It is not necessary for our purposes. It is quite enough if on the basis of what has been cited we can note the following:

If the dialectic is valid only for society, then it has the closest relationship to people, and L. admits this explicitly. (Rudas, *Arbeiterliteratur* IX, pp. 502–4)

22. Rudas writes:

But the unconscious intention of this objection on the part of L. is contained in the sentence where he reproaches the capitalist that 'his activity' is expended in the correct observation and calculation of the objective effect of social natural laws. It is probably true that in a communist society social natural laws will cease to be insoluble secrets, blind 'natural laws'. But what does the objective labour process of which Engels speaks have to do with the fact that it is like this in a capitalist society, and the capitalist restricts himself socially to observing these laws? The proletariat likewise observes these laws, only its calculation is better, for its point of view is not distorted by the capitalist perspective. But that has nothing to do with the fact that the capitalist, inasmuch as he participates in production without knowing what he is doing (that is seldom the case today, and if so, then, instead of him, it is done by an engineer), must strive to shape the process of production objectively and correctly. No capitalist is so stupid that, in order to make boot polish, he allows methods of production to be used that are completely inappropriate for that purpose. Here, in Engels, discussion is always about industry as an objective process of production, a metabolic exchange between person and nature, and not its capitalist husk. (Rudas, *Arbeiterliteratur* IX, pp. 515–16)

23. The questions Rudas poses of Lukács include: 'How does society get the dialectic that does not exist in nature? It must have arisen with society. (This conclusion is only untenable if society itself did not arise but was eternally there. Or if it existed prior to nature. In that case another question ensues: how did the dialectic cease to be in nature, which arose later than society?)'

24. For example, Rudas states in his first critical essay on Lukács:

. . . for a materialist, there are – according to Engels – 'things in themselves', i.e. an external world, which in part we do not know, and 'things for us', i.e. that part of the world which we already know. And the 'things in themselves' transform themselves constantly into 'things for us' in the process of praxis and knowledge. And if Marx speaks in the passage cited of a 'class for itself', then that is perfectly fine and not at all in opposition to the way that Engels uses this terminology, and he is certainly not using Hegel's terminology or even a weak echo of it. For it is clear that a class, if it possesses class consciousness, feels itself and knows itself to be a class, with class interests, in opposition to a hostile class. It is a class not only 'in itself', that is, objectively, according to its socio-economic characteristics, but also 'for itself' in its consciousness. For the class consists of people gifted with consciousness and this consciousness makes it possible that the class can achieve consciousness of itself too. But what does it mean to use the terminology 'for itself' in contrast to 'in itself' in the case of things, of the colouring matter of the madder or of alizarin? Can perhaps alizarin achieve consciousness of itself too? Can it become a 'thing in itself'? In Hegel, yes! In Engels and Marx, never! In L. it would seem also yes! Because he is also an idealist! ('Orthodoxe Marxismus?', in *Arbeiterliteratur* IX)

In the final part of his critique, he writes:

As in L., so in Adler: an antithesis is constructed between nature and 'nature'. They simply deny what anyone who has just taken one look at Marx and Engels knows: that Marx and Engels characterised their theory as a natural-scientific theory, that they did not rip into two nature and society, in order to construct an artificial antithesis, whereby society is tagged 'nature' in comparison with nature. Max Adler and Lukács, the new idealists, proceed no differently to those old new Hegelians, against whom Marx and Engels fought and whom they criticised along the same lines as one could criticise these:

'With this the relation of man to nature is excluded from history and hence the antithesis of nature and history is created.' (*German Ideology*, 'The Illusion of the Epoch') (Rudas, *Arbeiterliteratur* XII, pp. 1065–6)

25. Rudas complains:

. . . it is again disconcerting that Comrade L. assumes that the 'Hegel connoisseur' Engels did not know his Kant. That Kant was an agnostic is – despite the fact that Comrade L. challenges it – without doubt. According to Kant, we can on principle never know the world 'in itself'. Of course Comrade L. is correct to say that Kant maintained the complete discernibility of the world of appearances. But precisely because of that he was a *half*-materialist. The compromise character of Kantian philosophy was ascertained without question by Plekhanov and Lenin. To waste any more words on it here is pointless. But likewise, just as a thinker of the rank of Marx was aware of the far-reaching implications of everything he said or did, so too was a thinker of the rank of Kant. When he says: 'I had to abolish science in order to make room for belief' – then that was not empty talk on his part, or a concession to political powers (as some Kant-worshippers today now claim), but meant in all seriousness. He was not an agnostic on one single point: his ethics, his belief, in relation to the personality, which, representing simultaneously appearance and 'thing in itself', was – to use the words of Hegel–Lukács – a 'thing for itself'. In every other point Kant abolished science on principle: he was agnostic.

And in the passage quoted Engels speaks only of this agnosticism. He says: You, Kant, maintain – like all agnostics – that the world 'in itself', the 'things in themselves' are unknowable. But they are indeed knowable, inasmuch as we make them serve our purposes. In other words, he says the same as Marx says in the second thesis on Feuerbach:

'The question whether objective truth can be attributed to human thinking is not a question of theory but is a *practical question*. Man must prove the truth, i.e. the reality and power, the this-sidedness of his thinking in praxis. The dispute over the reality or non-reality of thinking that is isolated from praxis is a purely *scholastic* question.'

Engels says the same thing. And he does not mention one tiny little word about Kant not admitting the concrete expansion of our knowledge. Engels was aware of that just as well as anyone who has taken the briefest glance at Kant's work. But what Engels wanted to say against Kant was that this (practical and theoretical) expansion of our knowledge in the world of appearances is everything and beyond that there is nothing to know. That is to say, the world of appearances is everything, and the 'thing in itself' is a pure 'crochet', if we take it to mean not such things that we do not yet know, but can know, but rather things that we do not know and never can know. That is what Engels says, and nothing else. And Comrade L.'s objection would be, at best, a little carping, if it were not the fact that this carping meant not a challenge to Kant's agnosticism, but rather the defence of idealism and the 'correction' of materialism! (Rudas, *Arbeiterliteratur* IX, p. 511)

Georg Lukács as the philosopher of Leninism

Slavoj Žižek

Georg Lukács's *History and Class Consciousness* (1923) is one of the few authentic events in the history of Marxism. Today, we cannot but experience the book as the strange remainder of a bygone era – it is difficult even to imagine properly the traumatic impact its appearance had on generations of Marxists, including the later Lukács himself who, in his Thermidorian phase, i.e. from the early 1930s onwards, desperately tried to distance himself from it, to confine it to a document of merely historical interest, and conceded to its reprint only in 1967, accompanied by a new, long, self-critical introduction. Until this 'official' reprint, the book led a kind of underground spectral existence of an 'undead' entity, circulating in pirated editions among the German students in the 1960s, available in some rare translations (like the legendary French one from 1959). In my own country, the now defunct Yugoslavia, reference to *History and Class Consciousness* served as the ritualistic *signe de reconnaissance* of the entire critical Marxist circle around the journal *Praxis* – its attack on Engels's notion of the 'dialectics of nature' was crucial for the critical rejection of the 'reflection' theory of knowledge as the central tenet of 'dialectical materialism'. This impact was far from confined to Marxist circles: even Heidegger was obviously affected by *History and Class Consciousness*, since there are a couple of unmistakable hints at it in *Being and Time* – for instance, in the very last paragraph, Heidegger, in an obvious reaction to Lukács's critique of 'reification', asks the question: '[. . .] we know for a long time that there is the danger of "reifying consciousness". But what does reification [Verdinglichung] mean? Where does it originate from? [. . .] Is the "difference" between "consciousness" and "thing" at all sufficient for a fundamental deployment of the ontological problematic?"[1]

I

So how did *History and Class Consciousness* attain this cult status of a quasi-mythical forbidden book, comparable, perhaps, only to the no less traumatic impact of *Pour Marx*, written by Louis Althusser, Lukács's later great anti-Hegelian antipode?[2] The answer that first comes to one's mind is, of course, that we are dealing with the founding text of the entire tradition of Western Hegelian Marxism, with a book that combines an engaged revolutionary stance with topics that were later developed by the different strands of so-called critical theory up to today's cultural studies (the notion of 'commodity fetishism' as the structural feature of the entire social life, of 'reification' and 'instrumental reason', and so on). However, on a closer look, things appear in a slightly different light: there is a radical break between *History and Class Consciousness* – more precisely, between Lukács's writings from *c.* 1915 to *c.* 1930, inclusive of his *Lenin* from 1924, a series of his other short texts from this period not included in *History and Class Consciousness* and published in the 1960s under the title *Tactics and Ethics*, as well as the manuscript of the present volume, *Chvostismus und Dialektik*, Lukács's answer to his Comintern critics – and the later tradition of Western Marxism. The paradox (for our Western 'post-political' perspective) of *History and Class Consciousness* is that we have a philosophically extremely sophisticated book, a book that can compete with the highest achievements of the non-Marxist thought of its period, and yet a book that is thoroughly engaged in the ongoing political struggle, a reflection on the author's own radically Leninist political experience (among other things, Lukács was a minister of cultural affairs in the short-lived Hungarian Communist government of Bela Kun in 1919).[3] The paradox is thus that, with regard to the 'standard' Frankfurt School Western Marxism, *History and Class Consciousness* is at the same time much more openly politically engaged *and* philosophically much more speculative-Hegelian in character (see the notion of proletariat as the subject–object of history, a notion towards which members of the Frankfurt School always retained an uneasy distance) – if there ever was a philosopher of Leninism, of the Leninist party, it is the early Marxist Lukács who went to the very limit in this direction, up to defending the 'undemocratic' features of the first year of the Soviet power against Rosa Luxemburg's famous criticism, accusing her of 'fetishising' formal democracy, instead of treating it as one of the possible strategies to be endorsed or rejected with regard to the demands of a concrete revolutionary situation.[4] And what one should avoid today is precisely obliterating this aspect, reducing thereby Lukács to a gentrified and depoliticised cultural critic, warning about 'reification' and 'instrumental reason', motifs long ago appropriated even by the conservative critics of 'consumer society'.

So, precisely as the originating text of Western Marxism, *History and Class Consciousness* occupies the position of an exception, confirming yet again Schelling's notion that 'the beginning is the negation of that which begins with it'.[5] In what is this exceptional state grounded? In the mid-1920s, what Alain Badiou calls the 'Event of 1917' began to exhaust its potential, and the process took a Thermidorian turn. This term is to be conceived of not only in the usual Trotskyist way (betrayal of the revolution by a new bureaucratic class), but also in the strict sense elaborated by Badiou:[6] as the cessation of the Event, as the betrayal not of a certain social group and/or their interests, but of the fidelity to the (revolutionary) Event itself. In the Thermidorian perception, the Event and its consequences became unreadable, 'irrational', dismissed as a bad dream of the collective plunge into madness – 'we were all caught in a strange destructive vortex . . .'.

What then happened with the saturation of the 'revolutionary sequence of 1917' (Badiou) is that a direct theoretico-political engagement like that of Lukács in *History and Class Consciousness* became impossible. The socialist movement definitively split into social-democratic parliamentary reformism and the new Stalinist orthodoxy, while Western Marxism, which abstained from openly endorsing any of these two poles, abandoned the stance of direct political engagement and turned into a part of the established academic machine whose tradition runs from the early Frankfurt School up to today's cultural studies – therein resides the key difference that separates it from Lukács of the 1920s. On the other hand, Soviet philosophy gradually assumed the form of 'dialectical materialism' as the legitimising ideology of the 'really existing socialism' – one of the signs of the gradual rise of the Thermidorian Soviet orthodoxy in philosophy is precisely the series of vicious attacks on Lukács and his theoretical colleague Karl Korsch, whose *Marxism and Philosophy* is a kind of companion piece to *History and Class Consciousness*, even to the extent of being published in the same year (1923). The watershed for this development was the Fifth Congress of the Comintern in 1924, the first congress after Lenin's death, and simultaneously the first after it became clear that the era of revolutionary agitation in Europe was over and that socialism would have to survive in Russia on its own.[7] In his famous intervention at this Congress, Zinoviev afforded himself a rabble-rousing anti-intellectualist attack on the 'ultra-leftist' deviations of Lukács, Korsch and other 'professors', as he contemptuously referred to them, supporting Lukács's Hungarian Party companion László Rudas in the latter's critical rejection of Lukács's 'revisionism'. Afterwards, the main criticism of Lukács and Korsch originated in Abram Deborin and his philosophical school, at that time predominant in the Soviet Union (although later purged as 'idealist Hegelian'), who were the first systematically to develop the notion of Marxist philosophy as a universal dialectical method, elaborating general laws which can then be applied either to natural or to social phenomena – Marxist dialectics was thus deprived of its directly engaged, practical-revolutionary attitude, and turned into a general epistemological theory dealing with the universal laws of scientific knowledge.

As was noted already by Korsch in the aftermath of these debates, their crucial feature was that critiques from the Comintern and those from the 'revisionist' social-democratic circles, officially sworn enemies, basically repeated the *same* counter-arguments, being disturbed by the same theses in Lukács and Korsch, denouncing their 'subjectivism' (the practical-engaged character of Marxist theory, and so on). Such a position was no longer admissible at a time when Marxism was changing into a state ideology whose ultimate *raison d'être* was to provide the after-the-fact legitimation for the pragmatic political party decisions in ahistorical ('universal') laws of dialectics. Symptomatic here was the sudden rehabilitation of the notion that dialectical materialism was the 'world-view [Weltanschauung] of the working class': for Lukács and Korsch, as well as for Marx, a 'world-view' by definition designates the 'contemplative' stance of ideology with which Marxist revolutionary engaged theory has to break.

Evert Van der Zweerde has developed in detail the ideological functioning of the Soviet philosophy of dialectical materialism as the 'scientific world-view of the working class':[8] although it was a self-proclaimed ideology, the catch is that it was not the ideology it claimed to be – it did not motivate, but rather legitimated political acts; it was not to be believed in, but ritualistically enacted; the point of its claim to be 'scientific ideology' and thus the 'correct reflection' of social circumstances was to preclude the possibility that there could still be in Soviet society a 'normal' ideology which 'reflected' social reality in a 'wrong' way; and so on. We thus totally miss the point if we treat the infamous 'diamat' as a genuine philosophical system: it was an instrument of power legitimation to be enacted ritualistically, and, as such, to be located in the context of the thick cobweb of power relations. Emblematic here are the different fates of I. Ilyenkov and P. Losev, two prototypes of Russian philosophy under socialism. Losev was the author of the last book published in the USSR (in 1929) that openly rejected Marxism (discarding dialectical materialism as 'obvious nonsense'); however, after a short prison term, he was allowed to pursue his academic career and, during the Second World War, even started lecturing again – the 'formula' of his survival was that he withdrew into the history of philosophy (aesthetics) as a specialist scientific discipline, focusing on ancient Greek and Roman authors. Under the guise of reporting on and interpreting past thinkers, especially Plotin and other neo-Platonists, he was thus able to smuggle in his own spiritualist mystical theses while, in the introductions to his books, paying lip service to the official ideology by a quote or two from Khrushchev or Brezhnev. In this way, Losev survived all the vicissitudes of socialism and lived to see the end of communism, hailed as the grand old man of the authentic Russian spiritual heritage! In contrast to Losev, the problem with Ilyenkov, a superb dialectician and expert on Hegel, was that he was the eerie figure of a sincere Marxist–Leninist; for that reason (i.e. because he wrote in a personally engaging way, endeavouring to elaborate Marxism as a serious philosophy, not merely as a legitimising set of ritualistic formulae), he was gradually excommunicated and finally driven to suicide – was there ever a better lesson on how an ideology effectively functions?[9]

In a gesture of a personal Thermidor, Lukács himself, in the early 1930s, withdrew and turned to the more specialised areas of Marxist aesthetics and literary theory, justifying his public support of the Stalinist politics in the terms of the Hegelian critique of the Beautiful Soul: the Soviet Union, including all its unexpected hardships, was the outcome of the October Revolution, so, instead of condemning it from the comfortable position of the Beautiful Soul keeping its hands clean, one should bravely 'recognise the heart in the cross of the present' (Hegel's formula of the post-revolutionary reconciliation) – Adorno was fully justified in sarcastically designating this Lukács as someone who misread the clatter of his chains for the triumphant march forward of World Spirit, and, consequently, endorsed the 'extorted reconciliation' between the individual and society in the East European Communist countries.[10]

II

This fate of Lukács none the less confronts us with the difficult problem of the emergence of Stalinism: it is too easy to contrast the authentic revolutionary *élan* of the 'Event 1917' with its later Stalinist Thermidor – the true problem is 'how did we get from there to here?' As Alain Badiou has emphasised, the great task today is to think the necessity of the passage from Leninism to Stalinism without denying the tremendous emancipatory potential of the Event of October, i.e. without falling into the old liberal babble of the 'totalitarian' potential of radical emancipatory politics, on account of which every revolution has to end up in a repression worse than that of the old overthrown social order. The challenge to be faced here is the following one: while conceding that the rise of Stalinism is the inherent result of the Leninist revolutionary logic (not the result of some particular external corruptive influence, like the

'Russian backwardness' or the 'Asiatic' ideological stance of its masses), one should none the less stick to a concrete analysis of the logic of the political process and, at any price, avoid the recourse to some immediate quasi-anthropological or philosophical general notion like 'instrumental reason'. The moment we endorse this gesture, Stalinism loses its specificity, its specific political dynamic, and turns into just another example of this general notion (the gesture exemplified by Heidegger's famous remark, from his *Introduction to Metaphysics*, that, from the epochal historical view, Russian communism and Americanism are 'metaphysically the same').

Within Western Marxism, it was, of course, Adorno's and Horkheimer's *Dialectic of Enlightenment*, as well as Horkheimer's later numerous essays on the 'critique of instrumental reason', that accomplished this fateful shift from concrete socio-political analysis to philosophico-anthropological generalisation, the shift by means of which the reifying 'instrumental reason' is no longer grounded in concrete capitalist social relations, but itself almost imperceptibly becomes their quasi-transcendental 'principle' or 'foundation'. Strictly correlative to this shift is the almost total absence of theoretical confrontation with Stalinism in the tradition of the Frankfurt School, in clear contrast to its permanent obsession with Fascist anti-Semitism. The very exceptions to this rule are tell-tale: Franz Neumann's *Behemoth*, a study of national socialism which, in the typical fashionable style of the late 1930s and 1940s, suggests that the three great world systems – emerging New Deal capitalism, Fascism and Stalinism – tend towards the same bureaucratic, globally organised, 'administered' society; Herbert Marcuse's *Soviet Marxism*, his least passionate and arguably worst book, a strangely neutral analysis of the Soviet ideology with no clear commitments; and, finally, attempts by some Habermasians who, reflecting upon the emerging dissident phenomena, endeavoured to elaborate the notion of civil society as the site of resistance to the Communist regime – interesting politically, but far from offering a satisfactory global theory of the specificity of the Stalinist 'totalitarianism'.[11] The standard excuse – that the Frankfurt School classical authors did not want to oppose Communism too openly, since, by doing this, they would play into the hands of their domestic pro-capitalist cold-war warriors – is obviously insufficient: the point is not that this fear of being put in the service of official anti-communism proves how they were secretly pro-communist, but rather the opposite, for if they had been really cornered as to where they stood in the Cold War, they would have chosen Western liberal democracy (as Horkheimer explicitly did in some of his late writings). It was *this* ultimate solidarity with the Western system when it was really threatened that they were somehow ashamed to acknowledge publicly, in clear symmetry to the stance of the 'critical democratic socialist opposition' in the German Democratic Republic whose members criticised Party rule, but, the moment the situation became really serious and the socialist system was seriously threatened, they (Brecht *à propos* of the East Berlin workers' demonstrations in 1953, Christa Wolf *à propos* of the Prague Spring in 1968) publicly supported the system. 'Stalinism' (really existing socialism) was thus, for the Frankfurt School, a traumatic topic with regard to which it *had* to remain silent – this silence was the only way for them to retain their inconsistent position of its underlying solidarity with the Western liberal democracy without losing the official mask of its 'radical' leftist critique. Openly acknowledging this solidarity would have deprived the Frankfurt School theorists of their 'radical' aura, changing them into another version of the cold war anti-communist left liberals, while showing too much sympathy for 'really existing socialism' would have forced them to betray their unacknowledged basic commitment.

It is difficult not to be surprised by the unconvincing, 'flat' character of the standard anti-communist accounts of Stalinism with their references to the 'totalitarian' character of radical emancipatory politics, and so on – today, more than ever, one should insist that only a Marxist, dialectical-materialist, account can effectively explain the rise of Stalinism. While, of course, this task is far beyond the scope of the present essay, one is tempted to risk a brief preliminary remark. Every Marxist recalls Lenin's claim, from his *Philosophical Notebooks*, that no one who has not read and studied in detail Hegel's entire *Science of Logic* can really understand Marx's *Capital* – along the same lines, one is tempted to claim that no one who has not read and studied in detail the chapters on judgement and syllogism from Hegel's *Logic* can grasp the emergence of Stalinism. That is to say, the logic of this emergence can perhaps best be grasped as the succession of the three forms of syllogistic mediation which vaguely fit the triad of Marxism–Leninism–Stalinism. The three mediated terms (Universal, Particular and Singular) are History (the global historical movement), the Proletariat (the particular class with a privileged relationship to the Universal) and the Communist Party (the singular agent). In the first, classical Marxist, form of their mediation, the Party mediates between History and Proletariat: its action enables the 'empirical' working class to become aware of its historical mission inscribed into its very social position and to act accordingly, i.e. to become a revolutionary subject. The accent is here on the 'spontaneous' revolutionary stance of the proletariat: the Party only acts in a maieutic role, rendering possible the purely formal conversion of the proletariat from the Class-In-Itself to the Class-For-Itself.

However, as always in Hegel, the 'truth' of this mediation is that, in the course of its movement, its starting point, the presupposed identity, is falsified. In the first form, this presupposed identity is that between Proletariat and History, that is the notion that the revolutionary mission of universal liberation is inscribed in the very objective social condition of the proletariat as the 'universal class', as the class whose true particular interests overlap with the universal interests of humanity – the third term, the Party, is merely the operator of the actualisation of this universal potential of the particular. What becomes palpable in the course of this mediation is that the proletariat can 'spontaneously' achieve only trade-unionist reformist awareness, so we come to the (supposedly) Leninist conclusion: the constitution of the revolutionary subject is possible only when (those who will become) party intellectuals gain insight into the inner logic of the historical process and accordingly 'educate' the Proletariat. In this second form, the Proletariat is thus diminished to the role of the mediator between History (global historical process) and the scientific knowledge about it embodied in the Party: after gaining insight into the logic of historical process, the Party 'educates' workers into being the willing instrument of the realisation of the historical goal. The presupposed identity in this second form is that between Universal and Singular, between History and the Party, that is the notion that the Party as the 'collective intellectual' possesses effective knowledge of the historical process. This presupposition is best rendered by the overlapping of the 'subjective' and the 'objective' aspect: the notion of History

as an objective process determined by necessary laws is strictly correlative to the notion of party intellectuals as the Subject whose privileged
knowledge of, and insight into, this process allows it to intervene and
direct it. And, as one might expect, it is this presupposition that is falsified in the course of the second mediation, bringing us to the third,
'Stalinist', form of mediation, the 'truth' of the entire movement, in
which the Universal (History itself) mediates between the Proletariat
and the Party: to put it in somewhat simplistic terms, the Party merely
uses the reference to History – that is, its doctrine, 'dialectical and historical materialism', embodying its privileged access to the 'inexorable
necessity of the historical progress' – in order to legitimate its actual
domination over and exploitation of the working class, that is, to provide
the opportunistic pragmatic Party decisions with a kind of 'ontological
cover'.[12]

To put it in the terms of the speculative coincidence of the opposites,
or of the 'infinite judgement' in which the highest coincides with the
lowest, the fact that Soviet workers were awakened early in the morning
by the music from loudspeakers playing the first chords of the
Internationale whose words are 'Arise, you prisoners of work!' is granted a
deeper ironic meaning: the ultimate 'truth' of the pathetic original
meaning of these words ('Resist, break the chains that constrain you and
reach for freedom!') turns out to be its literal meaning, the call to the
tired workers 'Get up, slaves, and start working for us, the Party *nomenklatura!*'

III

So, back to the triple syllogistic mediation of History, the Proletariat and
the Party: if each form of mediation is the 'truth' of the preceding one
(the Party that instrumentalises the working class as the means to realise
its goal founded in the insight into the logic of the historical progress is the
'truth' of the notion that the Party merely enables the Proletariat to
become aware of its historical mission, that it only enables it to discover
its 'true interest'; the Party ruthlessly exploiting working classes is the
'truth' of the notion that the Party just realises through them its profound

insight into the logic of History), does this mean that this movement is inexorable, that we are dealing with an iron logic on account of which, the moment we endorse the starting point – the premise that the Proletariat is, as to its social position, potentially the 'universal class' – we are caught, with a diabolic compulsion, in a process at the end of which there is the Gulag? If this were the case, *History and Class Consciousness*, in spite of (or, rather, on account of) its intellectual brilliance, would be the founding text of Stalinism, and the standard postmodernist dismissal of this book as the ultimate manifestation of Hegelian essentialism, as well as Althusser's identification of Hegelianism as the secret philosophical core of Stalinism – the teleological necessity of the progress of the entire History towards the proletarian revolution as its great turning point, in which Proletariat as the historical Subject–Object, the 'universal class' enlightened by the Party about the mission inscribed into its very objective social position, accomplishes the self-transparent Act of liberation – would be fully justified. The violent reaction of the partisans of 'dialectical materialism' against *History and Class Consciousness* would again be an example of Lucien Goldmann's rule of how the ruling ideology necessarily has to disavow its true fundamental premises: in this perspective, the Lukácsian megalomaniac Hegelian notion of the Leninist Party as the historical Spirit embodied, as the 'collective intellectual' of the Proletariat qua absolute Subject–Object of History, would be the hidden 'truth' of the apparently more modest 'objectivist' Stalinist account of revolutionary activity as grounded in a global ontological process dominated by universal dialectical laws. And, of course, it would be easy to play against this Hegelian notion of Subject–Object the basic deconstructionist premise that the subject emerges precisely in/as the *gap* in the Substance (objective Order of Things), that there is subjectivity only in so far as there is a 'crack in the edifice of Being', only in so far as the universe is in a way 'derailed', 'out of joint', in short, that not only the full actualisation of the subject always fails, but that what Lukács would have dismissed as the 'defective' mode of subjectivity, as the thwarted subject, is effectively the subject itself.

The Stalinist 'objectivist' account would thus be the 'truth' of *History and Class Consciousness* also for strictly inherent philosophical reasons: since the subject is failed by definition, its full actualisation as the

Subject–Object of History necessarily entails its self-cancellation, its self-objectivisation as the instrument of History. And, furthermore, it would be easy to assert, against this Hegelo-Stalinist deadlock, the Laclauian postmodern assertion of radical contingency as the very terrain of (political) subjectivity: political universals are 'empty', the link between them and the particular content that hegemonises them is what is at stake in the ideological struggle which is thoroughly contingent, in other words, no political subject has its universal mission written in its 'objective' social condition.

Is, however, this effectively the case with *History and Class Consciousness*? Can Lukács be dismissed as the advocate of such a pseudo-Hegelian assertion of Proletariat as the absolute Subject–Object of History? Let us return to the concrete political background of *History and Class Consciousness*, in which Lukács still speaks as a fully engaged revolutionary. To put it in somewhat rough and simplified terms, the choice, for the revolutionary forces in the Russia of 1917, in the difficult situation in which the bourgeoisie was not able to bring to fruition the democratic revolution, was the following one.

On the one hand, the Menshevik stance was that of obedience to the logic of the 'objective stages of development': first the democratic revolution, then the proletarian revolution. In the whirlpool of 1917, instead of capitalising on the gradual disintegration of state apparatuses and building on the widespread popular discontent and resistance against the provisional government, all radical parties should resist the temptation to push the movement too far and rather join forces with democratic bourgeois elements in order first to achieve the democratic revolution, waiting patiently for the 'mature' revolutionary situation. From this point, a socialist take-over in 1917, when the situation was not yet 'ripe', would trigger a regression to primitive terror . . . (Although this fear of the catastrophic terrorist consequences of a 'premature' uprising may seem to augur the shadow of Stalinism, the ideology of Stalinism effectively marks a *return* to this 'objectivist' logic of the necessary stages of development.)[13]

On the other hand, the Leninist stance was to take a leap, throwing oneself into the paradox of the situation, seizing the opportunity and *intervening*, even if the situation was 'premature', with a wager that this very 'premature' intervention would radically change the 'objective' relationship of forces itself, within which the initial situation appeared as 'premature', that is, that it would undermine the very standards with reference to which the situation was judged as 'premature'.

Here, one must be careful not to miss the point: it is not that, in contrast to Mensheviks and sceptics among the Bolsheviks themselves, Lenin thought that the complex situation of 1917, that is the growing dissatisfaction of the broad masses with the irresolute politics of the provisional government, offered a unique chance of 'jumping over' one phase (the democratic bourgeois revolution), of 'condensing' the two necessary consecutive stages (democratic bourgeois revolution and proletarian revolution) into one. Such a notion still accepts the fundamental underlying objectivist 'reified' logic of the 'necessary stages of development'; it merely allows for the different rhythm of its course in different concrete circumstances (in other words, that in some countries, the second stage can immediately follow the first one). In contrast to this, Lenin's point is much stronger: ultimately, there is no objective logic of the 'necessary stages of development', since 'complications' arising from the intricate texture of concrete situations and/or from the unanticipated results of 'subjective' interventions always derail the straight course of things. As Lenin was keen on observing, the fact of colonialism and of the super-exploited masses in Asia, Africa and Latin America radically affects and 'displaces' the 'straight' class struggle in the developed capitalist countries – to speak about 'class struggle' without taking into account colonialism is an empty abstraction which, translated into practical politics, can result only in condoning the 'civilising' role of colonialism and thus, by subordinating the anti-colonialist struggle of the Asian masses to the 'true' class struggle in developed Western states, de facto accepts that the bourgeoisie defines the terms of the class struggle.[14] One is tempted to resort here to Lacanian terms: what is at stake in this alternative is the (in)existence of the 'big Other': the Mensheviks relied on the all-embracing foundation of the positive logic of historical development, while Bolsheviks (Lenin, at least) were aware that 'the big Other doesn't exist' – a political intervention proper does not occur within the coordinates of some underlying global matrix, since what it achieves is precisely the 'reshuffling' of this very global matrix.

This, then, is the reason that Lukács had such admiration for Lenin: his Lenin was the one who, *à propos* of the split in Russian social democracy between Bolsheviks and Mensheviks, when the two factions fought about a precise formulation of who could be a party member as defined in the party programme, wrote: 'Sometimes, the fate of the entire working class movement for long years to come can be decided by a word or two in the party programme.' Or the Lenin who, when he saw the chance for the revolutionary take-over in late 1917, said: 'History will never forgive us if we miss this opportunity!' At a more general level, the history of capitalism is a long history of how the predominant ideologico-political framework was able to accommodate – and to soften the subversive edge of – the movements and demands that seemed to threaten its very survival. For example, for a long time, sexual libertarians thought that monogamic sexual repression was necessary for the survival of capitalism – now we know that capitalism can not only tolerate, but even actively incite and exploit forms of 'perverse' sexuality, not to mention promiscuous indulgence in sexual pleasures. However, the conclusion to be drawn from it is *not* that capitalism has the endless ability to integrate and thus cut off the subversive edge of all particular demands – the question of timing, of 'seizing the moment', is crucial here. A certain particular demand possesses, at a specific moment, a global detonating power; it functions as a metaphoric stand-in for the global revolution: if we unconditionally insist on it, the system will explode; if, however, we wait too long, the metaphoric short-circuit between this particular demand and the global overthrow is dissolved, and the system can, with sneering hypocritical satisfaction, make the reply 'You wanted this? Here, have it!', without anything truly radical happening. The art of what Lukács called *Augenblick* – the moment when, briefly, there is an opening for an *act* to intervene in a situation – is the art of seizing the right moment, of aggravating the conflict *before* the system can accommodate itself to our demand. So we have here a Lukács who is much more 'Gramscian' and conjuncturalist/contingentian than is usually assumed – the Lukácsian *Augenblick* is unexpectedly close to what, today, Alain Badiou endeavours to formulate as the Event: an intervention that cannot be accounted for in the terms of its pre-existing 'objective conditions'. The crux of Lukács's argumentation is to reject the reduction of the act to its 'historical circumstances': there are no neutral 'objective conditions', or, in Hegelese, all presuppositions are already minimally posited.

Exemplary here is, at the very beginning of the present book, Lukács's analysis of the 'objectivist' enumeration of the causes of the failure of the Hungarian revolutionary council-dictatorship in 1919: the treason of the officers in the army, the external blockade that caused hunger . . . Although these are undoubtedly facts that played a crucial role in the revolutionary defeat, it is none the less methodologically wrong to evoke them as raw facts, without taking into account the way they were 'mediated' by the specific constellation of the 'subjective' political forces. Take the blockade: why was it that, in contrast to even stronger blockade of the Russian Soviet state, the latter did not succumb to the imperialist and counter-revolutionary onslaught? Because, in Russia, the Bolshevik Party made the masses aware of how this blockade is the result of foreign and domestic counter-revolutionary forces, while, in Hungary, the Party was ideologically not strong enough, so the working masses succumbed to the anti-Communist propaganda which claimed that the blockade was the result of the 'anti-democratic' nature of the regime – the logic of 'let's return to "democracy" and foreign aid will start to flow in . . .'. Treason of the officers? Yes, but why did the same treason not lead to the same catastrophic consequences in Soviet Russia? And, when traitors were discovered, why was it not possible to replace them with reliable cadres? Because the Communist Party was not strong and active enough, while the Russian Bolshevik Party mobilised properly the soldiers who were ready to fight to the end to defend the revolution. Of course, one can claim that the weakness of the Communist Party is again an 'objective' component of the social situation; however, behind this 'fact', there are again other subjective decisions and acts, so that we never reach the zero level of a purely 'objective' state of things – the ultimate point is not objectivity, but social 'totality' as the process of the global 'mediation' between the subjective and the objective aspects. In other words, the Act cannot ever be reduced to an outcome of objective conditions.

To take an example from a different domain, the way an ideology involves 'positing its presuppositions' is also easily discernible in the standard (pseudo)-explanation of the growing acceptance of the Nazi ideology in the Germany of the 1920s by the fact that the Nazis were deftly manipulating ordinary middle-class people's fears and anxieties generated by the economic crisis and fast social changes. The problem with this explanation is that it overlooks the self-referential circularity at work here: yes, the Nazis certainly did deftly manipulate fears and anxieties – however, far from being simple pre-ideological facts, these fears and anxieties were already the product of a certain ideological perspective. In other words, the Nazi ideology itself (co)generated 'anxieties and fears' against which it then proposed itself as a solution.

IV

We can now return again to our triple 'syllogism' and determine in what, precisely, resides its mistake: in the very opposition between its first two forms. Lukács, of course, is opposed to the 'spontaneist' ideology of advocating autonomous grass-roots self-organisation of the working masses against the externally imposed 'dictatorship' of the Party bureaucrats, as well as to the pseudo-Leninist (actually Kautsky's) notion that the 'empirical' working class can, on its own, reach only trade-unionist reformist level, and that the only way for it to become the revolutionary subject is that independent intellectuals gain a neutral 'scientific' insight into the 'objective' necessity of the passage from capitalism to socialism, and then import this knowledge into the empirical working class, 'educating' them about the mission inscribed into their very objective social position. It is here that we encounter the opprobrious dialectical 'identity of the opposites' at its purest: the problem with these oppositions is not that the two poles are too crudely opposed and that the truth is somewhere in between, in their 'dialectical mediation' (class consciousness emerges from the 'interaction' between spontaneous self-awareness of the working class and the educational activity of the Party); the problem is rather that the very notion that the working class has the inner potential to reach adequate revolutionary class consciousness (and, consequently, that the Party merely plays a modest, self-erasing, maieutic role of enabling the empirical workers to actualise this potential) legitimises the Party's exertion of dictatorial pressure over the 'empirical', actually existing workers and their confused, opportunistic self-awareness, in the name of (the Party's correct insight into) what their true inner potentials and/or their 'true long-term interests' in fact are. In short, Lukács is here simply applying to the false opposition between 'spontaneism' and external party domination the Hegelian speculative identification of the 'inner potential' of an individual with the external pressure exerted on him by his educators: to say that an individual possesses 'inner potential' to be a great musician is strictly equivalent to the fact that this potential has to be already present in the educator who, through external pressure, will compel the individual to actualise it.

So the paradox is that the more we insist on how revolutionary stance directly translates the true 'inner nature' of the working class, the more are we compelled to exert external pressure on the 'empirical' working class to actualise this inner possibility. In other words, the 'truth' of this immediate identity of the opposites, of the first two forms, is, as we have seen, the third form, the Stalinist mediation – why? Because this immediate identity precludes any place for the *act* proper: if class consciousness arises 'spontaneously', as the actualisation of inner potential inscribed into the very objective situation of the working class, then there is no real act at all, just the purely formal conversion from in-itself to for-itself, the gesture of bringing to light what was always-already there; if the proper revolutionary class consciousness is to be 'imported' via the Party, then we have, on the one hand, 'neutral' intellectuals who gain the 'objective' insight into historical necessity (without engaged *intervention* into it), and then what is ultimately their instrumental-manipulative use of the working class as the tool to actualise the necessity already written in the situation – again, no place for an *act* proper.

This notion of the act also enables us to deal with the feature that seems to justify fully the critical dismissal of Lukács as a determinist 'Hegelian' Marxist: his ill-famed distinction between empirical, factual, class consciousness (a phenomenon of collective psychology to be established via positive sociological research) and the 'attributed/ascribed/imputed (*zugerechnete*)' class consciousness (the consciousness that it is 'objectively possible' for a certain class to achieve if it fully mobilises its subjective resources). As Lukács emphasises, this opposition is not simply the opposition between truth and falsity: in contrast to all other classes, it is 'objectively possible' for the proletariat to achieve self-consciousness which allows it the correct insight into the true logic of the historical totality – it depends on the mobilisation of its subjective potential through the Party to what extent the factual working class will reach the level of this 'ascribed' class consciousness. In contrast to the proletariat, the 'imputed' consciousness of all other classes, although it also reaches beyond their factual consciousness, is not yet the true insight into the historical totality, but remains an ideological distortion (Lukács refers here to Marx's well-known analysis of the French Revolution of 1848 in which the cause of Napoleon III's '18th Brumaire' was that the radical bourgeoisie did not even fully actualise its own progressive political potential). The reproach imposes itself here almost automatically: does not Lukács himself implicitly regress to the Kantian opposition between the ideal formal possibility and the empirical factual state of things which always lags behind this ideal? And is not implicit in this lag the justification of the domination of the Party over the working class: the Party is ultimately precisely the mediator between the 'imputed' and the factual consciousness – it knows the potential ideal consciousness and endeavours to 'educate' the empirical working class to reach this level? If this were to be all that Lukács means by 'subjective mediation', by act and decision, then, of course, we would still remain within the confines of the 'reified' reliance on the 'objective stages of development': there is the prescribed ideal-typical limit of what is 'objectively possible', the limit of the 'ascribed' consciousness determined by the objective social position of a class, and all the manoeuvring space that is left to historical agents is the gap between this 'objectively possible' maximum and the extent to which they effectively approach this maximum.

There, is, however, another possibility open: to read the gap between factual and 'imputed' class consciousness not as the standard opposition between the ideal type and its factual blurred actualisation, but as the inner self-fissure (or 'out-of-jointness') of the historical subject. To be more precise, when one speaks of the proletariat as the 'universal class', one should bear in mind the strictly dialectical notion of universality which becomes actual, 'for itself', only in the guise of its opposite, in an agent who is out-of-place in any particular position within the existing global order and thus entertains towards it a negative relationship – let me quote here Ernesto Laclau's apposite formulation (thoroughly Hegelian notwithstanding Laclau's declared anti-Hegelianism):

> the universal is part of my identity in so far as I am penetrated by a constitutive lack – that is, in so far as my differential identity has failed in its process of constitution. The universal emerges out of the particular not as some principle underlying and explaining it, but as an incomplete horizon suturing a dislocated particular identity.[15]

In this precise sense, 'the universal is the symbol of a missing fullness':[16] I can relate to the Universal as such only in so far as my particular identity is thwarted, 'dislocated', only in so far as some impediment prevents me from 'becoming what I already am' (with regard to my particular social position). The claim that the proletariat is the 'universal class' is thus ultimately equivalent to the claim that, within the existing global order, the proletariat is the class that is radically dislocated (or, as Badiou would have put it, occupying the point of 'symptomal torsion') with regard to the social body: while other classes can still maintain the illusion that 'Society exists', and that they have their specific place within the global social body, the very existence of the proletariat repudiates the claim that 'Society exists'. In other words, the overlapping of the Universal and the Particular in the proletariat does *not* stand for their immediate identity (in the sense that the particular interests of the proletariat are at the same time the universal interests of humanity, so that the proletarian liberation will be equivalent to the liberation of the entire humanity): the universal revolutionary potential is rather 'inscribed into the very being of the proletariat' as its inherent radical split. This split, again, is not the immediate split between the particular interests/positions of the proletariat and its universal historical mission – the 'universal mission' of the proletariat arises from the way the proletariat's very particular existence is 'barred', hindered, from the way proletariat is a priori ('in its very notion', to put it in Hegelese) not able to realise its very *particular* social identity. The split is thus the split between the particular positive identity and the barrier, inherent blockage, that prevents the proletarians from actualising this very particular positive identity (their 'place in society') – only if we conceive of the split in this way, is there a space for the act proper, not only for the actions that follow universal 'principles' or 'rules' given in advance and thus providing the 'ontological cover' for our activity.

Therein resides the ultimate difference between, on the one hand, the authentic Leninist Party, and, on the other hand, the Kautskyist–Stalinist Party as embodying the non-engaged 'objective knowledge' which is to be imparted to the uneducated working class: the Kautskyist–Stalinist Party addresses the proletariat from a position of 'objective' knowledge intended to supplement the proletarian subjective (self)-experience of suffering and exploitation, i.e. the split here is the split between the proletarian 'spontaneous' subjective self-experience and the objective knowledge about one's social situation, while, in an authentic Leninist Party, the split is thoroughly subjective, that is, the Party addresses the proletariat from a radically subjective, engaged position of the lack that prevents the proletarians from achieving their 'proper place' in the social edifice.[17] And, furthermore, it is this crucial difference that also explains why the Stalinist sublime body of the Leader (with mausoleums and all the accompanying theatrics) is unthinkable within the strict Leninist horizon: the Leader can be elevated into a figure of Sublime Beauty only when the 'people' whom he represents is no longer the thoroughly dislocated proletariat, but the positively existing substantial entity, the 'working masses'.

To those whose reaction here is that what we are describing now is a hair-splitting philosophical distinction of no use to engaged fighters, let us recall a similar experience with Kant's practical philosophy: is it not that Kant's apparently 'difficult' propositions on the pure form of law as the only legitimate motif of an ethical act, and so on, suddenly become clear if we directly relate them to our immediate ethical experience? And the same goes for the above-mentioned distinction: the gap that separates reliance on the 'objective logic' from the risk of an authentic act is 'intuitively' known to anyone engaged in a struggle.

V

A further possible misunderstanding has to be clarified here: Lukács's position is not, as it may appear to a superficial reader, that the whole of history hitherto was dominated by 'reified' objective necessity, and that it is only with the late capitalist crisis, and the concomitant strengthening of the revolutionary proletarian stance, that the 'objective possibility' arises for the all-encompassing chain of necessity to be broken. All human history is characterised by the dialectical tension and interdependence between necessity and contingency; what one should be careful about is to distinguish different historical shapes of this interdependence. In pre-modern society, it was, of course, not only possible – it effectively happened all the time – that totally meaningless contingencies (the madness or some other psychological peculiarity of the monarch) could lead to global catastrophic consequences (like the utter destruction of rich and highly civilised Arab cities by the Mongols); however, psychological idiosyncrasies could have such consequences only within certain well-defined power relations and relations of production in which so much authority is effectively invested in the leader. In modern capitalist society, contingency reigns in the guise of the 'unpredictable' interplay of market forces which can 'for no apparent reason at all' instantly ruin individuals who worked hard all their life: as Marx and Engels already put it, the Market is the modern reincarnation of the ancient capricious Fate, in other words, this 'contingency' is the form of appearance of its dialectical obverse, of the impenetrable blind necessity of the capitalist system. Finally, in the revolutionary process, the space is open, not for a metaphysical foundational 'act', but for a contingent, strictly 'conjunctural', intervention that can break the very chain of Necessity dominating all history hitherto.

Exemplary is here Lukács's critique of the liberal sceptical attitude towards the October Revolution, which considers it as an important, but risky 'political experiment': the position of 'let's wait and patiently observe its final outcome . . .'. As Lukács is fully justified to retort, such an attitude transposes the experimental/observational stance of natural sciences on to human history: it is the exemplary case of observing a process from a safe distance, exempting oneself from it, not of the engaged stance of someone who – as always-already caught, embedded, in a situation – intervenes in it. Of course, Lukács's key point is here that we are not dealing with a simple opposition between the stance of impassive observation and the stance of practical intervention ('enough of words and empty theories, let's finally do something!'): Lukács advocates the dialectical unity/mediation of theory and practice, in which even the utmost contemplative stance is eminently 'practical' (in the sense of being embedded in the totality of social (re)production and thus expressing a certain 'practical' stance of how to survive in this totality), and, on the other hand, even the most 'practical' stance implies a certain 'theoretical' framework; it materialises a set of implicit ideological propositions. For example, the resigned 'melancholic' stance of searching for the meaning of life in withdrawn contemplative wisdom is clearly embedded in the historical totality of a society in decay, in which the public space no longer offers an outlet for creative self-affirmation; or, the stance of external observer who treats social life as an object in which one 'intervenes' in an instrumental-manipulative way and 'makes experiments', is the very stance required for the participation in a market society. On the other hand, the utmost individualistic stance of radical hedonism 'practises' the notion of man as a hedonistic being, that is, as Hegel would have put it, a person is never directly a hedonist, rather he relates himself to himself as one. In classical Marxist terms, not only is social consciousness a constitutive part of social being (of the actual process of social (re)production), but this 'being' itself (the actual process of social (re)production) can run its course only if mediated/sustained by the adequate form of 'consciousness': say, if, in a capitalist society, individuals are, in their daily practical lives, not prey to 'commodity fetishism', the very 'real' process of capitalist (re)production is perturbed. Here enters the crucial Hegelian notion of (self)-consciousness, which designates the gaining of self-awareness as an inherently *practical act*, to be opposed to the contemplative notion of a scientific 'correct insight': self-consciousness is an insight that directly 'changes its object', affects its actual social status – when the proletariat becomes aware of its revolutionary potential, this very 'insight' transforms it into an *actual* revolutionary subject.

In so far as (self)-consciousness designates the way things appear to the subject, this identity of thought and being in the practical act of self-consciousness can also be formulated as the dialectical identity of Essence and its Appearance. Lukács relies here on Hegel's analysis of the 'essentiality' of appearance: appearance is never a 'mere' appearance, it belongs to the essence itself. This means that consciousness (ideological appearance) is also an 'objective' social fact with an effectivity of its own: as we already pointed out, bourgeois 'fetishistic' consciousness is not simply an 'illusion' masking actual social processes, but a mode of organisation of the very social *being*, crucial to the actual process of social (re)production.[18]

Lukács here can be said to participate in the great 'paradigm shift' at work also in quantum physics, and whose main feature is not the dissolution of 'objective reality', its reduction to a 'subjective construction', but, on the contrary, the unheard-of assertion of the 'objective' status of the appearance itself. It is not sufficient to oppose the way things 'objectively are' to the way they 'merely appear to us': the way they appear (to the observer) affects their very 'objective being'. This is what is so path-breaking in quantum physics: the notion that the limited horizon of the observer (or of the mechanism that registers what goes on) determines what effectively goes on. We cannot say that self-awareness (or colour or material density or . . .) designate merely the way we experience reality, while 'objectively' there are only subatomic particles and their fluctuations: these 'appearances' have to be taken into account if we are to explain what 'effectively is going on'. In a homologous way, the crux of Lukács's notion of class consciousness is that the way the working class 'appears to itself' determines its 'objective' being.[19]

It is of crucial importance not to misread Lukács's theses as another version of the standard hermeneutic opposition between *Erklären* (the explanatory procedure of the natural sciences) and *Verstehen* (the form of comprehension at work in the human sciences): when Lukács opposes the act of self-consciousness of a historical subject to the 'correct insight' of natural sciences, his point is not to establish an epistemological distinction between two different methodological procedures, but, precisely, to break up the very standpoint of formal 'methodology' and to assert that *knowledge itself is part of social reality*. All knowledge, of nature and of society, is a social process, mediated by society, an 'actual' part of social structure, and, on account of this self-referential inclusion of knowledge into its own object, a revolutionary theory is ultimately (also) its own meta-theory. Although Lukács was adamantly opposed to psychoanalysis, the parallel with Freud is here striking: in the same way, psychoanalysis also interprets the resistance against itself as the result of the very unconscious processes that are its topic, Marxism interprets the resistance against its insights as the 'result of the class struggle in theory', as accounted for by its very object – in both cases, theory is caught in a self-referential loop; it is, in a way, the theory about the resistance to itself.

However, a further, even more fateful, misunderstanding would be to read this thesis on the social mediation of every form of knowledge as the standard historicist assertion of how each form of knowledge is a social phenomenon, 'a child of its age', dependent upon and expressing the social conditions of its emergence. Lukács's point is precisely to undermine this false alternative of historicist relativism (there is no neutral knowledge of 'objective reality', since all knowledge is biased, embedded in a specific 'social context') and of the distinction between the socio-historical conditions and the inherent truth-value of a body of knowledge (even if a certain theory emerged within a specific social context, this context provides only external conditions, which in no way diminish or undermine the 'objective truth' of its propositions – for example, although, as everyone knows, Darwin elaborated his evolutionary theory under the stimulus of Malthus's economics, Darwinism is still acknowledged as true, while Malthus is deservedly half-forgotten). As he puts it in *History and Class Consciousness*, the problem of historicism is that it is not 'historicist' enough: it still presupposes an empty external observer's point *for* which and *from* which all that happens is historically relativised. Lukács overcomes this historicist relativisation by bringing it to its conclusion, that is by way of including in the historical process the observing subject itself, thus undermining the very exempted measure with regard to which everything is relativised: the attainment of self-consciousness of a revolutionary subject is *not* an insight into how its own stance is relativised, conditioned by specific historical circumstances, but a practical act of *intervening* into these 'circumstances'.[20] Marxist theory describes society from the engaged standpoint of its revolutionary change and thereby transforms its object (the working class) into a revolutionary subject – the neutral description of society is formally 'false', since it involves the acceptance of the existing order. Far from 'relativising' the truth of an insight, the awareness of its own embeddedness in a concrete constellation – and thereby of its engaged, partial, character – is a positive condition of its truth.

And therein resides the great achievement of the present manuscript: in *Chvostismus und Dialektik*, Lukács sets the record straight with regard to the possible misreadings of his basic position as articulated in *History and Class Consciousness*, not only against its obvious target, the emerging pseudo-Leninist Soviet orthodoxy that was later sanctified in the guise of the Stalinist 'Marxism–Leninism', but – for us today even more importantly – against the already mentioned predominant Western reception of *History and Class Consciousness* focused on the fashionable motif of 'reification'. When, in *Chvostismus*, Lukács elaborates in detail the passing critical remarks on Engels's notion of the 'dialectics of nature' from *History and Class Consciousness*, he makes it clear that his critique of the 'dialectics of nature' is embedded in his more fundamental critique of the notion of the revolutionary process as determined by the 'objective' laws and stages of historical development. The point of Lukács's polemics against the 'dialectics of nature' is thus not the Kantian abstract-epistemological one (the notion of 'dialectics of nature' misrecognises the 'subjective mediation' of what appears as natural reality, i.e. the subjective constitution of – what we perceive as – 'reality'), but ultimately a *political* one: the 'dialectics of nature' is problematic because it legitimises the stance towards the revolutionary process as obeying 'objective laws', leaving no space for the radical contingency of *Augenblick*, for the *act* as a practical intervention irreducible to its 'objective conditions'.

And today, in the era of the worldwide triumph of democracy when (with some notable exceptions like Alain Badiou) no leftist dares to question the premises of democratic politics, it is more crucial than ever to bear in mind Lukács's reminder, in his polemics against Rosa Luxemburg's critique of Lenin, as to how the authentic revolutionary stance of endorsing the radical contingency of the *Augenblick* should also not endorse the standard opposition between 'democracy' and 'dictatorship' or 'terror'. The first step to make, if we are to leave behind the opposition between liberal-democratic universalism and ethnic/religious fundamentalism on which even today's mass media focus, is to acknowledge the existence of what one is tempted to call 'democratic fundamentalism': the ontologicisation of democracy into a depoliticised universal framework which is not itself to be (re)negotiated as the result of politico-ideological hegemonic struggles. Lukács is well aware that the qualification of the 'dictatorship of the proletariat' as the 'democratic rule of the wide working classes, directed only against the narrow circle of ex-ruling classes' is a simplistic sleight of hand: the Bolsheviks, of course, often *did* break the democratic 'rules of the game', we *did* experience the Bolshevik 'Red Terror'.

Democracy as the form of state politics is inherently 'Popperian': the ultimate criterion of democracy is that the regime is 'falsifiable', that is, that a clearly defined public procedure (the popular vote) can establish that the regime is no longer legitimate and must be replaced by another political force. The point is not that this procedure is 'just', but rather that all parties concerned agree in advance and unambiguously upon it irrespective of its 'justice'. In their standard procedure of ideological blackmail, defenders of state democracy claim that the moment we abandon this feature, we enter the 'totalitarian' sphere in which the regime is 'non-falsifiable', that is, it forever avoids the situation of unequivocal 'falsification': whatever happens, even if thousands demonstrate against the regime, the regime continues to maintain that it is legitimate, that it stands for the true interests of the people and that the 'true' people support it . . . Here, we should *reject* this blackmail (as Lukács does *à propos* of Rosa Luxemburg): there are no 'democratic (procedural) rules' one is a priori prohibited to violate. Revolutionary politics is not a matter of 'opinions', but of the truth on behalf of which one often *is* compelled to disregard the 'opinion of the majority' and to impose the revolutionary will against it. In the difficult times of the foreign intervention and civil war after the October Revolution, Trotsky openly admitted that the Bolshevik government was ready sometimes to act against the factual opinion of the majority – not on behalf of a privileged 'insight into objective truth', but on behalf of the very 'subjective'

tension between the fidelity to the Revolutionary Event and the opportunistic retreat from it, the tension that is inherent to the revolutionary
process itself. (Significantly, although Stalinism was factually a much
more violent dictatorship, it would never openly acknowledge acting
against the opinion of the majority – it always clung to the fetish of the
People whose true Will the Leadership expresses.) The political legacy of
Lukács is thus the assertion of the unconditional, 'ruthless' revolutionary
will, ready to 'go to the end', effectively to seize power and undermine
the existing totality; its wager is that the alternative between authentic
rebellion and its later 'ossification' in a new order is not exhaustive, in
other words, that revolutionary effervescence should take the risk of
translating its outburst into a New Order. Lenin was right: after the revolution, the anarchic disruptions of the disciplinary constraints of
production should be replaced by an even stronger discipline. Such an
assertion is thoroughly opposed to the 'postmodern' celebration of the
good 'revolt' as opposed to bad 'revolution', or, in more fashionable
terms, of the effervescence of the multitude of marginal 'sites of resistance' against any actual attempt to attack the totality itself (see the mass
media's depoliticising appropriation of the May 1968 events as an 'outburst of spontaneous youthful creativity against the bureaucratised mass
society').[21]

As Alain Badiou repeatedly emphasises, an Event is fragile and rare – so
instead of merely focusing on 'how did the October Revolution turn into
a Stalinist Thermidor?', we should perhaps turn the question around: is
it the Thermidorian forswearing of the Event, the passive following of
the course of things, that appears as 'natural' to the human animal? The
big question is rather the opposite one: how is it possible that, from
time to time, the impossible miracle of an Event does take place at all
and leaves traces in the patient work of those who remain faithful to it?
So the point is not to 'develop further' Lukács in accordance with the
'demands of new times' (the great motto of all opportunist revisionism,
up to New Labour), but to *repeat* the Event in new conditions. Are we still
able to imagine ourselves a historical moment when terms like
'revisionist traitor' were not yet parts of the Stalinist mantra, but
expressed an authentic engaged insight?

In other words, the question to be asked today *à propos* of the unique Event of the early Marxist Lukács is not: 'How does his work stand in relation to today's constellation? Is it still alive?', but, to paraphrase Adorno's well-known reversal of Croce's patronising historicist question about 'what is dead and what is alive in Hegel's dialectic' (the title of his main work):[22] how do *we today* stand in relation to – in the eyes of – Lukács? Are we still able to commit the *act* proper, described by Lukács? Which social agent is, on account of its radical dislocation, *today* able to accomplish it?

Notes

1. Martin Heidegger, *Sein und Zeit* (Tübingen: Max Niemeyer Verlag, 1963), p. 437.

2. Let me evoke here again my personal experience: roughly, one could say that, in the last two decades of the Communist regime, two philosophical orientations dominated intellectual life in Slovenia: Heideggerianism among the opposition and Frankfurt-school Marxism among the 'official' Party circles. So one would have expected the main theoretical fight to have taken place between these two orientations, with the third block – us, Lacanians and Althusserians – in the role of innocent bystanders. Yet, as soon as polemics broke out, both major orientations ferociously attacked the same particular third author, Althusser. In the 1970s, Althusser actually functioned as a kind of symptomatic point, a name *à propos* of which all the 'official' adversaries, Heideggerians and Frankfurt-Marxists in Slovenia, Praxis-philosophers and central-committee ideologues in Zagreb and Belgrade, suddenly started to speak the same language, pronouncing the same accusations. From the very beginning, the starting point of the Slovene Lacanians was this observation of how the name 'Althusser' triggered an enigmatic uneasiness in all camps. One is even tempted to suggest that the unfortunate event in Althusser's private life (his strangling of his wife) played the role of a welcome pretext, of a 'little piece of reality' enabling his theoretical adversaries to repress the real trauma represented by his theory ('How can a theory of somebody who strangled his wife be taken seriously?'). This resistance to Althusser, whose very excessive, almost 'irrational', character was deeply symptomatic, certified how it was precisely the Althusserian theory – defamed as proto-Stalinist – that served as a kind of 'spontaneous' theoretical tool for effectively undermining the Communist 'totalitarian' regimes: his theory of the Ideological State Apparatuses assigned the crucial role in the reproduction of an ideology to 'external' rituals and practices with regard to which 'inner' beliefs and convictions are strictly secondary. And is it necessary to call attention to the central place of such rituals in 'really existing socialism'? What counted in it was external obedience, not 'inner conviction' – obedience coincided

with the semblance of obedience, which is why the only way to be truly 'subversive' was to act 'naïvely', to make the system 'eat its own words', i.e. to undermine the appearance of its ideological consistency.

Paradoxically, from the perspective of each of these two Marxists, Althusser and Lukács, the other appears as the quintessential Stalinist: for Althusser and post-Althusserians, Lukács's notion of the Communist Party as the quasi-Hegelian Subject legitimises Stalinism; for the followers of Lukács, Althusser's structuralist 'theoretical anti-humanism', his rejection of the entire problematic of alienation and reification, plays into the hands of the Stalinist disregard for human freedom. While this is not the place to engage in detail in this confrontation, suffice it to emphasise how each of the two Marxists does articulate a crucial problematic excluded from the opponent's horizon: in Althusser, it is the notion of Ideological State Apparatuses as the material existence of ideology, and in Lukács, the notion of the historical act. And, of course, there is no easy way to accomplish a 'synthesis' between these two mutually exclusive approaches – perhaps the way to proceed would be via the reference to Antonio Gramsci, the other great founding figure of Western Marxism.

3. *History and Class Consciousness* thus marks a radical break also from the early pre-Marxist Lukács himself, whose main work, *A Theory of the Novel*, belongs to the Weberian tradition of socio-cultural criticism – no wonder that, in this book, he signed his name Georg von Lukács!

4. Of course, if one accepts to play alternative history games, one can safely surmise that, if Lenin were to have read *History and Class Consciousness*, he would have rejected its philosophical premises as 'subjectivist' and contrary to 'dialectical materialism' with its 'reflection' theory of knowledge (it is already significant how, in order to maintain his Leninist credentials, Lukács has virtually to ignore Lenin's *Materialism and Empiriocriticism*). On the other hand, in Lenin's entire writings, there is only one mention of Lukács: in 1921, in a brief note for the journal *Kommunismus*, the organ of the Comintern for south-eastern Europe, Lenin intervenes in a debate between Lukács and Bela Kun, ferociously attacking Lukács's text as 'very leftist and very bad. In it, Marxism is present only at a purely verbal level' (see V.I. Lenin, *Complete Works* [Russian edition], vol. 41, pp. 135–7). However, this is no way undermines the claim that Lukács is the ultimate philosopher of Leninism: it was rather Lenin himself who was not fully aware of the philosophical stance he 'practised' in his revolutionary work, and who only gradually (through reading Hegel during the First World War) became aware of it. The other key question, of course, is: was this misrecognition of one's true philosophical stance necessary for one's political engagement? In other words, does the rule, established already by Lucien Goldmann, in his classic *The Hidden God*, *à propos* of Pascal and the Jansenists (who were also unacceptable for the ruling Catholic circles), of how the ruling ideology necessarily has to disavow its true fundamental premises, apply also to Leninism? If the answer is 'yes', if the Leninist misrecognition of its philosophical premises is structurally necessary, then Leninism is just another ideology and Lukács's account of it, even if true, is insufficient: it can penetrate to the true philosophical premises of Leninism, but what it cannot explain is the very gap between

180   A DEFENCE OF *HISTORY AND CLASS CONSCIOUSNESS*

truth and appearance, i.e. the necessary disavowal of the truth in the false (objectivist, ontological, 'dialectical materialist') Leninist self-consciousness – as Lukács himself knows very well (this is one of the great Hegelian theses of *History and Class Consciousness*), appearance is never merely appearance, but is, precisely as appearance, essential.

5. F.W.J. Schelling, *Sämtliche Werke*, ed. K.F.A. Schelling (Stuttgart: Cotta, 1856–61), vol. VIII, p. 600.

6. See Chapter 9 of Alain Badiou, *Abrégé de métapolitique* (Paris: Seuil, 1998).

7. Incidentally, the lesson of these early years of the October Revolution is ultimately the same as that of today's post-Maoist China: contrary to the liberal ideologists, one has to assert that there is no necessary link between market and democracy. Democracy and market go together only with stable property relations: the moment they are perturbed, we get either dictatorship *à la* Pinochet's Chile or a revolutionary explosion. That is to say, the paradox to be emphasised is that, in the hard years of 'war communism' prior to the application of the New Economic Politics (NEP) which opened up the space again for market 'liberalisation', there was much more democracy in Soviet Russia than in the years of the NEP. The market liberalisation of the NEP goes hand-in-hand with the emergence of the strong party of *apparatchiks* gaining control over society: this party arose precisely as a reaction to the autonomy of the market civil society, out of the need to establish a strong power structure in order to control these newly unleashed forces.

8. See Evert van der Zweerde, *Soviet Historiography of Philosophy* (Dordrecht: Kluwer, 1997).

9. Paradigmatic here is the legendary story of Ilyenkov's failed participation at a world philosophy congress in the USA in the mid-1960s: Ilyenkov had already been given a visa and was set to take a plane, when his trip was cancelled because his written intervention, 'From the Leninist Point of View', which he had to present in advance to the Party ideologues, displeased them – not because of its (wholly acceptable) content, but simply because of its style, of the engaged way in which it was written; already the opening sentence ('It is my personal contention that . . .') struck a wrong chord.

10. See Theodor W. Adorno, 'Erpresste Versöhnung', in *Noten zur Literatur* (Frankfurt: Suhrkamp, 1974), p. 278.

11. See, as a representative example, Andrew Arato and Jean L. Cohen, *Civil Society and Political Theory* (Cambridge, MA: MIT Press, 1994).

12. What makes Fidel Castro's famous statement 'Within the Revolution, everything. Outside it, nothing!' problematic and 'totalitarian' is the way its radicality covers up its total indeterminacy: what it leaves unsaid is who, and based on what criteria, will decide if a particular artistic work (the statement was formulated to provide the guideline for dealing with artistic freedom) effectively serves the revolution or undermines it. The way is thus open for the *nomenklatura* to enforce its arbitrary decisions. (There is, however, another possible reading which may redeem this slogan: revolution is not a process that follows predestined 'laws', so there are no a priori objective criteria that

would allow us to draw a line of separation between the revolution and its betrayal – fidelity to the revolution does not reside in simply following and applying a set of norms and goals given in advance, but in the continuous struggle to redefine again and again the line separation.)

13. Let us also not forget that, in the weeks before October Revolution, when the debate was raging between Bolsheviks, Stalin did take sides against Lenin's proposal for an immediate Bolshevik take-over, arguing, along Menshevik lines, that the situation was not yet 'ripe', and that, instead of such dangerous 'adventurism', one should endorse a broad coalition of all anti-Tsarist forces!

14. Again, one can discern here the unexpected closeness to the Althusserian notion of 'overdetermination': there is no ultimate rule that allows one to measure 'exceptions' against it – in real history, there are, in a way, nothing but exceptions.

15. Ernesto Laclau, 'Universalism, Particularism, and the Question of Identity', *October* 61, p. 89.

16. Ibid.

17. Perhaps, a reference to Kierkegaard might be of some help here: this difference is the one between the positive Being of the Universal (the 'mute universality' of a species defined by what all members of the species have in common) and what Kierkegaard called the 'Universal-in-becoming', the Universal as the power of negativity that undermines the fixity of every particular constellation. For a closer elaboration of this distinction, see Chapter 2 of Slavoj Žižek, *The Ticklish Subject* (London: Verso, 1999).

18. In a more detailed approach, one would have to elaborate here this key Hegelian notion of the essentiality of appearance. Hegel's point is not the standard platitude that 'an essence has to appear', that it is only as deep as it is wide–expressed–externalised, etc., but a much more precise one: essence is, in a way, its own appearance, it appears *as essence* in the domain of appearance, i.e. essence is *nothing but* the appearance of essence, the appearance that there is something behind which is the Essence.

19. Here also, it would be interesting to establish the connection between Lukács and Badiou, for whom 'appearance' is the domain of the consistency of positive 'hard reality', while the order of Being is inherently fragile, inconsistent, elusive, accessible only through mathematics which deals with pure multitudes (see Chapter 14 of Alain Badiou, *Court traité d'ontologie transitoire* (Paris: Editions du Seuil, 1998). Although Lukács and Badiou are far from deploying the same notion of appearance, what they do have in common is the way both turn around the standard metaphysical opposition between Appearance and Being, in which appearance is transitory, in contrast to the hard positivity of Being – with Lukács, 'appearance' stands for the 'reified' objective reality, while the true 'actuality' is that of the transitory movement of subjective mediation. The homology with quantum physics again imposes itself: in the latter, what we experience as 'reality' is also the order of consistent 'appearance' that emerges through the collapse of quantum fluctuation, while the order of Being is that of the transitory, substanceless quantum fluctuations.

20. The same criticism could also be made apropos of Richard Rorty's notion that there is no objective truth, just a multitude of (more or less effective) stories about ourselves that we narrate to ourselves: the problem with this notion is not that it is too relativistic, but that it is not 'relativistic' enough – in a typically liberal way, Rorty still presupposes a non-relative neutral universal framework of rules (respect for others' pain, etc.) that everyone should respect when indulging in their own idiosyncratic way of life, the framework that guarantees the tolerable co-existence of these ways of life.

21. See, as exemplary of this stance, Kristeva's statements: 'today the word "revolt" has become assimilated to Revolution, to political action. The events of the twentieth century, however, have shown us that political "revolts" – Revolutions – ultimately betrayed revolt, especially the psychic sense of the term. Why? Because revolt, as I understand it – psychic revolt, analytic revolt, artistic revolt – refers to a state of per- manent questioning, of transformation, change, an endless probing of appearances. If we look at the history of political revolts, we see that the process of questioning has ceased . . . in the case of the Russian Revolution, a revolution that became increasingly dogmatic as it stopped questioning its own ideals until it ultimately degenerated into totalitarianism' (Julia Kristeva, 'The Necessity of Revolt', *Trans* 5, 1998, p. 125). One is tempted to add sarcastically to this last thesis: were not the great Stalinist or Khmer Rouge purges the most radical form of the political regime's 'permanent questioning'? More seriously, what is problematic with this position of depoliticising the revolt is that it precludes any actual radical political change: the existing political regime is never effectively undermined or overturned, just endlessly 'questioned' from different mar- ginal 'sites of resistance', since every actual radical change is in advance dismissed as inevitably ending up in some form of 'totalitarian' regression. So what this celebration of the 'revolt' effectively amounts to is the old reactionary thesis of how, from time to time, the existing order has to rejuvenate itself with some fresh blood in order to remain viable, like the vulgar conservative wisdom that every good conservative was in his youth briefly a radical leftist . . .

22. See Theodor W. Adorno, *Drei Studien zu Hegel* (Frankfurt: Suhrkamp, 1963), p. 13.